Routledge Revivals

The Payment of Wages

First published in 1928, *The Payment of Wages* came out amid the controversies over workshop conditions caused by the Great War. It has held its place as the standard work describing the various systems of wage payments and their effects. Mr. Cole raises challengingly the question of the need for a completely new policy on the part of the trade unions and employees alike. This book is sure to provoke discussion, and would be of interest to students of economy and history.

The Payment of Wages

A Study in Payment by Results Under the Wage System

G. D. H. Cole

First published in 1928
By George Allen & Unwin Ltd

This edition first published in 2023 by Routledge
4 Park Square, Milton Park, Abingdon, Oxon, OX14 4RN
and by Routledge
605 Third Avenue, New York, NY 10017

Routledge is an imprint of the Taylor & Francis Group, an informa business

Publisher's Note
The publisher has gone to great lengths to ensure the quality of this reprint but points out that some imperfections in the original copies may be apparent.

Disclaimer
The publisher has made every effort to trace copyright holders and welcomes correspondence from those they have been unable to contact.

A Library of Congress record exists under LCCN: 28030257

ISBN: 978-1-032-54310-9 (hbk)
ISBN: 978-1-003-42432-1 (ebk)
ISBN: 978-1-032-54325-3 (pbk)

Book DOI 10.4324/9781003424321

THE PAYMENT OF WAGES

A STUDY IN PAYMENT BY RESULTS UNDER THE WAGE-SYSTEM

By G. D. H. COLE

NEW AND REVISED EDITION

LONDON: GEORGE ALLEN & UNWIN, LTD.
RUSKIN HOUSE, 40 MUSEUM STREET, W.C.1
1928

SINGULARLY little has been published in this country on the questions dealt with in this book. So far as I know, there has been no general book on the question of wage-payment since Mr. D. F. Schloss's *Methods of Industrial Remuneration*, while there has never been a book dealing with the problem from the Trade Union point of view. In this preliminary study I have to acknowledge the very great help which I have received from many prominent Trade Unionists and officials. I may also add that this book was written at the instance of the Labour Research Department, and that the task of writing it would have been impossible without the very valuable collection of Trade Union materials which the Department has accumulated. I have particularly to thank Mr. W. H. Hutchinson of the Executive Council of the Amalgamated Society of Engineers for reading the book through in manuscript, and for making a number of valuable suggestions.

G. D. H. COLE.

June 1918.

ANYONE who compares the list of books appended to the present edition of this book with that of 1918 will see that the position has radically changed since I wrote the above preface. So large is the mass of books now dealing with the question that I have been able to select only a few of the most important.

For the present edition I have, in addition to writing the new chapter which now opens the book, made minor changes and corrections throughout. I have to thank numerous friends for pointing out errors and suggesting ways in which the book could be improved.

G. D. H. C.

OXFORD, *January* 1928.

CONTENTS

APPENDICES

PRELIMINARY CHAPTER TO THE EDITION OF 1928

The Payment of Wages was written during the Great War, amid the rapid changes in industrial practice which the war had made inevitable. But now that I come to revise it nine years later, I find something to add, but relatively little to alter. Industrial conditions have changed in many respects; but the fundamental problems of the wage-system remain the same. Indeed, the whole process of change has been a good deal slower than at one time seemed likely. There has been no wholesale shifting over from time-work to "payment by results," and even less a general adoption of "Scientific Management" in any of its various forms. Undoubtedly in certain industries, especially engineering, "payment by results" has made some further encroachments on the time-work system, and the war-time methods of standardisation have been to some extent permanently applied. Undoubtedly, too, the study known as "Industrial Psychology" has made some real headway, not only in the laboratory, but also as a practical contribution to workshop management. But the changes, taken as a whole, are not really extensive; and over most industries work still continues to be done and paid for largely under the conditions which prevailed when this book was written.

In certain respects, indeed, industry is less standardised now than in 1918; for during the latter stages of the war the need for vast supplies of uniform clothing, shells, fuses, and all manner of military equipment combined with the acute shortage of labour to promote the utmost possible use of standardised machinery and methods of mass-production. When the war ended, this great uniform demand ceased, and industries had to go back to an attempt to satisfy the far more diversified needs of the individual consumer. The great bodies of unskilled labour which had been brought together for war-time production were rapidly disbanded; special-purpose machines, unadaptable to the new needs, and even whole factories built up for specialised production of munitions of war, were extensively scrapped; and there was a rapid return in many industries to the productive methods which had been in force before the outbreak of war. Contrary to the general expectation, the Trade Union rules which had been suspended in order to increase war-time output were for the time restored in most cases with very little friction or reluctance.

This "restoration of pre-war practices" was, however, never quite complete. And, when it had been accomplished, a contrary tendency soon began to assert itself. Big manufacturers began to work out, on the basis of their war-time experience, methods of standardising operations required under the new industrial conditions, and to extend anew the use of semi-skilled labour on "foolproof" machinery of new types. That this process was relatively slow was due to the fact that the forms of standardisation had to be worked out afresh, and that it was far harder to apply mass-production methods to the more widely diversified output now called for by the conditions of demand.

Indeed, in the industries whose technique was most changed by war-time experience the changes often made little difference in the forms and methods of wage-payment. The iron and steel trades, for example, introduced great economies in the use of fuel, increased the size of the normal industrial unit, and thus reduced their costs of production especially by economising in the amount of labour employed. But these changes hardly affected the system of wage-payment. The tonnage system was applied unaltered to the new conditions of production. The engineering trades used less skilled and more semi-skilled and unskilled labour; but, while this increased the proportion of workers employed under some system of "payment by results," it did not cause any fundamental alteration in the methods of payment applied to the majority of workers in the skilled trades, among whom the time-workers were, even before the war, chiefly found.

Certain other industries, notably the whole range of textile trades, had been hardly affected at all by the war in their methods of production or wage-payment; and in these no great change has occurred even now. They remain predominantly piece-work industries, in which the great majority of the workers are paid wages corresponding exactly with their individual output. Even the building industry, though it has experienced a great standardisation of its products, has not so far changed much in its methods of production or wage-payment. There has been much ado about the "Weir houses," and the application of factory methods of mass-production to the building of workers' dwellings; but this has been mostly talk. The more important practical changes in the building industry centre round the growth of concrete houses, and the increased importance of the constructional engineer in the erection of the larger buildings. And neither of these changes has yet radically affected the methods of wage-payment. Building still remains pre-eminently a time-work industry.

Undoubtedly, the process of change would have been far more rapid but for the great depression which has affected British industry since 1921. The short-lived trade boom of 1919 and 1920 was a boom of prices and not of production ; and by the time factories were ready to increase their output and begin cutting their costs by the application of new methods the great slump was already on its way. It is obvious, however, that standardisation only pays, in most cases, when the reduction of costs opens up the prospect of a rapidly widening market. The British employer of 1921 and the following years could, as a rule, see no prospect of a sufficient growth of demand for his products to make mass-production a profitable policy. For a time, he was more disposed to use his power, acquired through war-time combination under Government control, for the purpose of restricting output in the hope of maintaining prices at a paying level. Such a policy was inconsistent with any drastic changes in the methods of production, for it would only pay to sink capital in new standardised machinery if a greatly extended market could be secured. The uncertainty of the international situation, the wildly fluctuating currencies of the principal industrial countries, the depressed life-standard of the workers in Germany and elsewhere, made any venture on these lines little better than a gamble, so far as the foreign market was concerned ; while the openness of the home-market to goods produced under the prevailing conditions abroad made any attempt to concentrate on stimulating home demand an exceedingly hazardous enterprise. Consequently, most manufacturers went on producing in the ways to which they had been accustomed ; and the revolution in productive methods, promised as the inevitable result of war-time experience, largely failed to materialise.

The Trade Unions, on their side, weakened by unemployment and with all their efforts concentrated on the struggle against lower wage-rates and the threat of a return to a longer working week, were not in a position to make any advance. The shop stewards' movement broke down abruptly when the conditions which had been the secret of its strength ceased to exist. No longer did " dilution " call for ceaseless changes in workshop practice ; no longer was labour so scarce as to be able largely to dictate its own terms. The active shop steward either lost his job as workers became plentiful, or was driven by prudence and necessity to moderate his activity in face of the changed conditions. The employer, weakened in his contest for profits in the markets of the world, was immensely strengthened in his relations with the workers. The powers of foremen and managers revived ; and the *de facto* control of the workshops, largely established by the skilled craftsmen under war conditions, was rapidly taken away.

If the employers had wished to revolutionise the conditions of production, to make " payment by results " universal, to adopt generally the methods of " Scientific Management," they had certainly a matchless opportunity for doing these things during the earlier years of the great slump. If they did not do them, it was because they did not want to do them—because they had no faith in their results. We have all been given, during the past few years, a signal example of this unwillingness in the case of the coal industry. The new pits in South Yorkshire and elsewhere are, indeed, worked by methods radically different from those which prevail over the industry as a whole. The differences are so great that a collier migrating from, say, Durham to Doncaster, has practically to learn a new craft when he is confronted with the coal-cutting machinery and the methods of organisation of the new pits. But, despite a whole sequence of Royal Commissions and Committees, the greater part of the coal industry is still working under the technique of pre-war days, and obstinately resisting adaptation even in pits which could be brought under new and more productive methods. Many of the older pits are doubtless incapable of adaptation; but will anyone maintain that the industry as a whole has done its best to bring its methods up to date?

Adoption of new technique is, of course, largely a matter of capital expenditure. It involves the scrapping of existing plants in which capital has been sunk, even when these plants are still capable of working—at a price. It involves the provision of new capital to replace the old; and this in turn involves a belief among masters that the new capital will yield an adequate return. In most industries, this belief has not existed, and therefore the new capital has not been applied. In some, notably in the chemical trades, in the artificial silk industry, and in the production of motor-cars, the belief has been created, the capital has been provided, and the technique of production has been revolutionised. And in these industries we find relatively high profits and wages, and a low rate of unemployment. Elsewhere, stagnation still prevails, especially in the great exporting trades to which we have long been used to look as the main sources of British prosperity.

Under these conditions, it has become fashionable to look for the means of salvation to the United States, where production has been immensely increased, and the standard of life considerably raised, while Great Britain has been standing still. Travellers fare forth to this new land of promise, and bring back word of its abounding prosperity. Everyone wants to master America's "secret," in order that we may imitate its results in our own industries. But different observers find the "secret" of America's advance in different things. One tells us that it is all because American workers impose no restrictions on output; another says it is because American wages are high, and therefore provide a vast and expansible home market; yet another attributes it to America's great natural resources, another to her tariff, and another to the fact that she is the largest free-trade area in the world.

These explanations concern us here only in so far as they have a bearing upon the question of wage-payment. It is often alleged that the American workmen produce more because, among them, "payment by results" is the prevailing system. But is it?

Certainly some of the largest and most successful factories in the United States are run mainly on a basis of time-work. Mr. Henry Ford places far less reliance on piece-work incentives than on setting, by means of standardisation, a factory pace to which the worker has to conform. The worker either does his work at this pace, or he goes, by resignation or dismissal. The "labour turnover" at the Ford factories is notoriously high. Mr. Ford owes his high output, first to the system of factory organisation which he has enforced, and secondly to the fact that his high time-wages constantly attract enough workers prepared to conform even to the killing pace which he sets.

Mr. Ford at least cannot, then, be used as an example for proving the benefits of "payment by results." And, if there are in America not wanting examples of high output obtained under this system, is it not plausible to seek rather an explanation which will cover all the cases than one which his experience seems to contradict?

"Payment by results," regarded as an incentive to higher output, is obviously most likely to succeed where the pace of production is directly under the workers' control. But in some modern forms of "mass-production" this is but little the case. The pace of work is set by the machine, as when the work is built up by a succession of minute and specialised operations performed by different workers as it passes them on a moving platform. At such jobs the worker must either stick the pace or go. It is useless to offer piece-work incentives, which will secure different responses from different workers. What is needed is a high uniform rate of work which all will observe. In order to get men to do this it is necessary to offer them a special inducement; but the appropriate inducement is a high time-rate, and not a piece-work price.

It would not be surprising, therefore, if it were found in this country, as in the United States, that some forms of standardised mass-production lead not to "payment by results," but to high time-rates combined with an exceptionally severe workshop discipline. Such high rates, of course, are relative. The rate need not be high absolutely, provided it is enough higher than the worker can get elsewhere to compensate him for the additional severity and disagreeableness of the conditions. There are already factories in England which are following Ford methods without paying Ford wages. Such a factory, set up in a low-wage area, may pay no more than the ordinary rates current in the great industrial districts, and yet secure all the "speeding up" that its owners can desire. The cheap motor factory, here as in America, is the chosen home of these methods. They are, however, still exceptional, even in the trades into which they have been introduced.

It may be taken as certain that the British employer will not get harder work without, in the long run at least, paying more for it in some form. The workman will not expend more effort except in return for an increased reward. This may take the form either of higher piece-work or bonus earnings, or of a higher time-rate; but in the one form or the other the additional payment will be successfully demanded. The same condition does not, of course, apply when higher output is secured by means of improvements in technique which do not make the workers' task harder or more unpleasant. Nor, even where the work is much harder, does it follow that the increased reward will be proportionate to the increased output secured. The labour cost of production, it is notorious, often falls in the factories when high wages are given in return for exceptionally hard or unremitting toil.

This doctrine of the "economy of high wages" has received, of late years, new and unexpected support. It used to be said that it applied only to the worst paid types of workers: that a rise in their case might yield a more than corresponding increase in productivity, but that, once a "living wage" had been secured, the worker would lose his readiness to respond to increasing doses of payment. The American evidence certainly does not seem to square with this view. The factories producing at lowest unit cost are, save perhaps in the textile trades, those which pay the highest wages, and this remains true long after the "living wage," in the common sense of the term, has been considerably exceeded.

It may be answered that this is not because the worker responds to the stimulus of higher wages, but because the factory is organised so as to compel him to produce more. This is largely true; but the American manufacturers have come to realise that the "economy of high wages" has another aspect besides that which is usually considered. The American employer pays more because he cannot get men to work at the pace he wants except by doing so. But, when he has paid his high wage in return for high output, he comes to realise that the high wage is itself the means through which the high output finds a market. This is concealed from the British employer, both because he is not subject to conditions which compel him to pay a high wage, and because his eyes are on the foreign more than on the home market. The "economy of high wages," therefore, has not hitherto appealed to his imagination. He still tries to cut his costs of production mainly, not by increasing output, but by reducing wage-rates and piece-work prices. He has still to realise that high output will not help him unless the workers' wages are high enough to enable them to buy it.

When this book was written, it seemed as if the main battle of the future would be fought between the rival systems of time-work and "payment by results." But now it is necessary to modify this view. The battle will be between those forms of higher production which place an additional strain upon the worker and make him even more than to-day an automaton divorced from all real control of the process on which he is engaged, and those which aim at an increased technical efficiency of a sort which will lighten labour and, at the least, not add to its monotony or to the rigidity of the discipline under which it is carried on. On the one side, we shall have more and more self-acting mechanisms which compel the worker, willy nilly, to go the pace set by the factory controllers, and thus render mere piece-work incentives obsolete. And on the other we shall have an increasing demand that the job be made to fit the man, instead of the man being crucified to fit the job.

It is in this second connection that the development of Industrial Psychology and Industrial Physiology will prove, in the long run, of the greatest importance. The earlier forms of "Scientific Management" studied men's physique and motives only in order to discover how to extract more out of them. Piece-work and bonus systems were so designed as to appeal to the worker to put forth every available ounce of effort; time-study and motion-study were used so as to provide the management with the means of drilling the reluctant workers into the most productive motions and postures. The object throughout was not to lighten labour, but to speed up the productive process.

Yet even these studies had in them the germ of better things. For, if productive effort was to be increased, it was necessary for wasteful effort to be eliminated. It was necessary to adapt the machine to the man, as well as the man to the machine, and to study the causes as well as the mere phenomena of industrial fatigue. It was essential to take into account the waste and friction which arose from the worker's distaste for his job, as well as the merely physical hindrances to its effective performance. The original motive in all these cases was doubtless to increase output and to lower its cost; and this motive is still predominant. But with it is increasingly mingled, especially in the minds of the scientists who carry on the work of investigation, the desire to make labour less irksome and unhealthy as well as more productive.

This is the good side of Scientific Management, and especially of its later developments in the field of Industrial Psychology and Industrial Physiology. The trouble is that the employer still controls industry, and the scientist, however he may theorise, can as a rule only influence industrial practice as the employer's servant, and subject to his veto. And the employer will usually spend money in carrying out the scientist's recommendations only if he can see in them a direct and immediate prospect of lowering the cost of production. Of indirect benefits, arising from greater mental and physical contentment, and less *malaise,* among his employees, the average employer is still apt to be decidedly sceptical.

Nor, of course, is he without warrant for this attitude. Industrial Psychology is still in its infancy, and a great many very foolish things are still proposed and done in its name. It can hardly advance as yet with safety beyond the simplest applications of common sense. But it is a great step forward that the question, "How do the workers feel about it?" should now be commonly asked in relation to industrial processes, and some attempt be made, by careful and exact investigation, to discover the answer.

A great deal that passes under the name of "Industrial Psychology" is, of course, in one sense not psychology at all. The expert psychologist who visits a works for the purpose of reporting on its methods is often concerned mainly with problems that are far more physiological than psychological. The way to smoother working may be, in many cases, the removal of an unnecessary physical strain which can be done away with by some simple adaptation of the machine, or by the provision of seats at an appropriate height, or by the institution of rest-pauses. Doubtless, such changes have important mental as well as physical results; but probably in the majority of cases a physical trouble is at the back of the mental *malaise* which the psychologist sets out to remove.

This new profession of "Industrial Psychologist" cannot preserve a strict impartiality above the industrial battle. The psychologist and the efficiency engineer will, as their respective techniques advance, become more and more able to tell how industry ought to be organised in order to achieve a given result. But they cannot give clear or decisive advice unless the desired result is defined in advance. Now, under existing conditions, there is no real agreement as to the result that is to be sought. The employer wants primarily higher output at lower unit cost; the worker wants primarily a reduction in the strain and unpleasantness of labour. To a greater extent than either party is commonly prepared to understand, the two aims can be harmonised; for in many cases the worker will work better and produce more if the conditions of production are made less distasteful. The advanced employer has already found this out; but employers who act on this principle are still few and far between.

Moreover, no complete harmony is attainable on this basis. It is not true that all employers who aim at reducing the unpleasantness of labour will do better than all who, ignoring the humanity of their workers, drive them hard under a relentless factory discipline of the Ford type. There are two rival ways of getting the most out of labour, and neither is inherently and universally superior to the other from a purely profit-making point of view. Indeed, some forms of mass-production go so against the human grain of labour as to be workable at all only on the latter method. It is impossible to look only to the progressively enlightened selfishness of the employer as the means of improving factory conditions.

The desire to get the highest possible output at the lowest cost and the desire to secure decent and, as far as may be, pleasant working conditions are often opposed in fact. Still more often, they seem to be opposed; and in practice it is their seeming that counts. If the industrial psychologist is to intervene in industry merely as the employer's servant, and if the adoption of his proposals is to depend merely on the employer's will, he will inevitably put first, or seem to put first, considerations of output, and relatively disregard, or seem to disregard, the worker's ease and convenience, whenever the two considerations conflict. The moral is obvious. If Industrial Psychology, in the wide sense currently given to the term, is destined to play a rapidly growing part in the determination of workshop conditions, it must be as much at the call of the workers as of the employers.

This is not, in practice, at all an easy result to secure. The Institute of Industrial Psychology does, indeed, aim at impartiality, and follows it to the extent of having seriously offended several big employers who have called upon it for advice. But it cannot escape the consequences of being almost wholly dependent on the employers' money, on the employers' initiative in calling it in, and on the employers' will in accepting or ignoring its recommendations. Though various prominent Trade Unionists are loosely associated with it, hardly a Trade Union yet takes it seriously, or sees the need for any close association with its doings. To no Trade Union has it yet occurred that the retention of an expert staff of its own is a necessary condition of successful collective bargaining under modern conditions, or that mere grumbling at the innovations of advanced managements is no substitute for intelligent criticism of their doings. Trade Unionism is, in most industries, a full generation behind the times in its methods of handling workshop problems. It is still following for the most part the rule of thumb methods which are being rapidly superseded among the more progressive members of the employing class and the managerial staffs of industry.

In the later chapters of this book, the reader will find a plea for some attempt by the Trade Unions at collective control of the problems of wage-payment. The matter has become a good deal more urgent now than it was nine years ago ; but next to nothing has been done to deal with it. Nowadays, indeed, the need is wider as well as more urgent. It is obvious that, unless British industry can radically improve its methods of production, the outlook is black for workman as well as for employer. It is no less obvious that the radical changes which will have to be made will deeply affect the whole position of the workers in the industrial system. They may be such as to reduce the operative more than ever to a condition of servitude to the machine, and to deprive him of all prospect of finding in labour anything save an almost intolerable irksomeness and restraint ; but they may also be such as to create for him an essentially co-operative relationship with management, and to place him in a position to insist that the conditions of production shall be made consistent with the human needs of the producer. They will certainly not issue in the latter result unless the Trade Unions, his representatives, are prepared to make themselves masters of the problems of industrial technique, and to play a creative and responsible part in the re-making of industry to meet the new needs.

America, that land of contracts, shows us both forces at work side by side. We are accustomed to believe that American Trade Unionism is half a century behind our own, and that the affairs of Capital and Labour are conducted in the United States in a spirit of barbarism which we civilised peoples have outlived. There is truth in the indictment; but it is only half the truth. While a large body of American employers is still in full cry for the "Open Shop," and American courts of justice are often prepared to gaol a Trade Union organiser for the mere crime of helping the workers to combine, there are also in the United States examples of Trade Union activity which the British Unions would do well to mark and inwardly digest. For more than one American Trade Union has seen the necessity of equipping itself with a properly trained expert staff, and of endeavouring with expert aid to play its part in the shaping of the policy and technique of industry. The Amalgamated Clothing Workers' Union, the most advanced and successful Trade Union in the United States, has by this means raised the needle industry from a grossly sweated occupation to a status envied by many of the most highly skilled crafts. And, in the locomotive shops of the Baltimore and Ohio Railroad, there has existed since 1922 a scheme of organised co-operation between the Trade Unions and the management which gives the workers, through their Unions, an effective and creative voice in the shaping of industrial policy. The Unions, guided by their own expert staff, take a real share in determining how the railway shops are to be run.

Objection is often taken to schemes of this sort on the ground that they involve the workers in some measure of responsibility for the conduct of industry under the capitalist system. But those who make this objection are in reality only running away from the problem. It is not to the workers' interest that capitalism should be inefficient. The present inefficiency of British industry actually strengthens the British capitalist against the British worker. Trade Unions can do most for their members when industry is booming and labour fully employed. Even revolutions are easier made on full than on empty stomachs. And it will most certainly not suit the British worker at all for British industry to decline. As it declines, wages will fall and unemployment will increase, with the result that the Trade Unions will be less than ever able to defend the interests of their members.

Trade Unionists have, therefore, a direct and personal interest in promoting the reorganisation of British industry, even under private control. If they want it transferred to public ownership, will it not be better transferred in good-going trim than as a bankrupt concern? Their interest is to help in making it more efficient, and, in doing so, to shape its development according to their own needs and ideas. Collaboration on these lines implies no surrender to capitalism, and no abandonment of the right to strike. It is actually a phase in the workers' struggle for power, and a means of building up a real system of democratic industrial control.

In any such policy as I am here advocating, the problem of wage-payment will occupy an important place. But it will be, far less than when this book was written, isolable from the general problems of factory organisation and industrial technique. "Payment by results" has made its appeal to employers as an incentive to higher output; and it is, as we have seen, already losing some of its appeal as alternative methods of increasing output are devised. At present, the choice of employers is in the main confined to the two alternatives of bribing their workers to produce more by piece-work inducements, or driving them either by strict supervision or by running the machinery at a speed to which they have to conform. These, however, are not the only possible alternatives; for both have been largely based on the assumption—true in the main under present conditions—that the worker is concerned to speed down rather than up. The enlistment of the worker as a co-operative agent in the stimulation of higher production—on terms which would ensure to him both a fairer reward and a productive method less irksome and disregardful of his feelings—would create an entirely new situation.

If, however, the employer desires this result, he must be prepared to pay the price. The workers will not implement, or the Trade Unions approve and forward, a policy of co-operation unless the co-operation is real. Whitleyism, paying lip-service to the idea of joint control, but in fact reserving all power in the employers' hands, will not do. Its failure has been proved already. Nor will those plans do which are based on the "loyalty" of the worker to the firm that employs him, and demand from him, as a condition of co-operation, acceptance of capitalism as a system claiming his allegiance. Worker and employer have a common interest in the promotion of more efficient productive methods; but they can never become allies, because a vital part of the worker's indictment of things as they are is that a large share of the existing inefficiency is traceable to capitalism itself. In co-operating for the increase of workshop efficiency, the worker will not be giving up his desire and intention to replace capitalism by a better system. Indeed, his co-operation will count, in his mind, as a step towards that replacement. In helping the employer to produce better, he will be also learning to do without the employer altogether.

If the Trade Unions are minded to follow the policy here outlined, it is evidently their business to take all industrial knowledge as their province, and above all to make themselves masters of the vital problems of workshop technique. They must be able not only to negotiate scientifically about piece-work prices, the definition of a "fair day's work," the degree of skill and effort required in the performance of the various industrial operations, the problems of fatigue and monotony in labour, and all the other matters which are now dealt with by industrial psychologists and " efficiency " experts, but also to meet the employers on equal terms in the discussion of improved methods of production, the introduction of new machines and processes, the scientific construction of workshops and factories, the routing of jobs from stage to stage, and all the other vital problems of factory management. The Trade Union must have, for all these things, experts of its own as skilled as those of the employer, and must be prepared, equally with the employer, to retain at need and pay for the services of the skilled consultant.

Unless Trade Unionism can adapt itself to these new needs, I would not give much for its chance of effective survival. It is surely obvious that old-style Trade Union policies are played out. As long as Great Britain could look for an almost automatic increase of wealth through the growth of her foreign trade, the Unions could be sure of getting something for their members merely by watching out for favourable opportunities of bringing pressure to bear upon the employers. But those days are past. Under present conditions, Britain's industrial wealth will increase only through better organisation, a more skilled use of machinery and science, and a more economical application of labour to the processes of production. It is no longer a case of waiting for the employer to get richer, and then claiming some of his riches from him ; the wealth of the future will have to be earned by co-operative effort of the whole body of producers.

I still adhere to the view, stated in the following chapters, that in the main the right line of advance is not the progressive substitution of individual " payments by results " for time-work, but rather that of collective for individual systems of payment. The method known as " collective contract " seems to me still the most hopeful method of organising that responsible relationship of the workers to industry which present conditions imperatively require.

In this connection, considerable importance attaches to the undoubted success, within a limited field, of the method of wage-payment known as the " Priestman-Atkinson " system. The basis of this arrangement is the payment to all workers employed in a factory or department of a collective bonus proportionate to any increase in output above a fixed standard. At the outset, this standard is determined in relation to the past experience of the factory. The output is classified into definite groups, and the number of " man-hours " of labour expended is calculated for these groups. In this calculation, all labour is reduced to man-hours of standard labour, an hour of a less skilled man's work being regarded as a fraction of the skilled man's hour, in accordance with their respective wage-rates. By these means, a standard output per standard man-hour is fixed for the factory or department as a whole, the labour of non-productive and indirectly productive workers, as well as that of direct producers, being included in the total. Staff workers, such as foremen and managers, are, however, usually excluded from the calculation.

The standard being thus fixed, the whole of the workers in the factory or department are paid, over and above their Trade Union wage-rates, which are guaranteed, a bonus proportionate to the amount by which the actual output of the factory or department per "man-hour" exceeds the standard. Thus, if output per "man-hour" rises by twenty per cent, the wages paid to the workers are increased by twenty per cent throughout the factory or department, the firm, of course, making its saving by the reduction of overhead costs. The system is usually, and best, applied in a factory where time-work is the basis of individual payment. It could also be applied in conjunction with individual piece-work, the piece-worker usually receiving the collective bonus on his piece-work earnings as well as on his time-rate. There would, however, be a considerable risk that the co-operative spirit which it is the object of the system to promote would be undermined by giving it this individualistic basis.

In its pure form, this system has, of all the existing systems of "payment by results," the most to recommend it. It does not set man against man, but treats the whole of the workers in the factory or department as an essentially co-operative group. It does away with the need for rate-fixing, and with most of the grounds that are constantly arising over the pricing or timing of jobs under the piece-work or premium bonus systems. It gives the workers a collective interest in improving the efficiency of production, and in removing causes of workshop friction. And it provides a basis on which the collective intervention of the workers in the problems of industrial technique and workshop control can be readily organised.

At the same time, too much is claimed for the system by some of its advocates. It does not, as some of them are inclined to assert, do away with the need for collective bargaining in the workshop. The fixing of the standard output per "man-hour" is a highly intricate business, on which the workers need expert advice and representation. Moreover, when the basis has been fixed, occasion is bound to arise for varying it. The type of product and the methods of manufacture, as well as the types of labour employed on various jobs, are bound to change over long periods at any rate; and each change will demand some readjustment of the standards on which the scheme is based. Here again, then, will be need for collective bargaining, and for the presence on the workers' side of experts able to meet those of the employers on equal terms.

While, however, it is no more true of the "Priestman-Atkinson" system than of the Taylor system that it removes the need for collective bargaining and strong Trade Union organisation in the workshop, there seems little doubt that, for many industries, the former method does supply both the best chance of securing increased output at lower cost and the easiest means for the workers of extending their control over industry in precisely those things which they are best equipped to control.

Of course, any such system as that described above implies—what is by no means always the case—that increased output is actually desired. The employer, however, under present conditions, is often no less eager to restrict output than to increase it. He wants the worker to increase his output per "man-hour," in order that the cost of production may be lowered; but he is often in some sort of ring or combine with other employers to "regulate" the total output of his industry, and bound down by the ring to a fixed quota which he is not allowed to exceed. In such cases, if the workers under the "Priestman-Atkinson" or any similar system increase their output per "man-hour," the employer will have to meet the situation either by dismissing some of the workers or by putting the works as a whole on short time. Now, it needs no argument to show that a body of workers, faced with this result of increasing their output, will be most unlikely and unwilling to do so, whatever incentives may be offered to them. It follows that the system of restriction of total output by rings of employers, while it may sometimes be effective in maintaining prices, inevitably makes against efficient production. It does this both because it disposes the worker to speed down, and also because it often does not pay to install the most up-to-date and productive machinery save with a view to a considerable expansion of output. The rapid growth in recent years of this form of restriction has undoubtedly been one of the most serious obstacles to the improvement both of industrial technique and of the productive efficiency of labour.

This serves to give point to my final contention—that above all the problem of wage-payment is a human problem. The essential characteristics of a satisfactory system of remuneration—for as long as we continue to think in terms of remuneration at all—are, first, that it shall put men in a mood to give of their best; secondly, that it shall not set one man's hand against another's, and thirdly, that it shall be, as far as possible, consistent with the sense of justice of those employed under it. But in none of these respects can the methods of wage-payment be considered, in practice, apart from the general systems of factory organisation and from the policies which inspire the owners and managers of the factories. The best system may fail if it is badly administered, or if the policy of the management engenders a bad state of feeling among the workers. Men labouring under a grievance will not work well, even if the payment is fair and fairly computed. Men will not produce more if the result is to be the throwing out of work of their friends and neighbours. Men will not strive to be more efficient for a management which wrecks the results of their work by bad administration, or for foremen who constantly antagonise them by their bullying and hostility. Above all, the employer who sets himself up against the Trade Union as a focus for the workers' loyalty, and seeks to establish in his works an oasis of patriarchal contentment, must expect to find his efforts constantly thwarted by the counter-pull of Trade Union loyalty. There is no reason why he should not work with the Trade Union, and co-operate with it in trying to establish good conditions and productive efficiency. If he will not do this, he has only himself to blame when matters go wrong.

It will be seen that, while I am keenly critical of many of the present developments of Scientific Management and Industrial Psychology, I have none the less great hopes of them for the future. Rightly handled, they are capable of doing an infinite deal both to increase production, and so raise the standard of life, and to lighten labour and make it go less against the grain, and so sweeten the temper and increase the happiness of the ordinary man. But these results depend on the great new powers which the application of science to industrial management promises to confer upon the world being used in the right way. They will not be rightly used if the main motive behind their application is the increase of private profit. They must be applied also, and even primarily, for the lessening of the "disvalue" of factory labour. It is above all for this reason that it is urgent for the organised workers to obtain a command and an understanding of the new forces, if only, for the time, in order to counteract their wrong use by employers intent only on private gain. And, as it is largely round the problems of wage-payment that the controversy will centre, it is on this point that the Trade Unions should in the first instance focus a good deal of their attention. At this point they must seek "control," and in order to seek control they must first of all seek more abundant and scientific knowledge.

CHAPTER I

INTRODUCTORY

THE following chapters are an attempt to describe a particular aspect of the wage system. Under the existing industrial system every worker has his price and receives his payment for service rendered, and one of the most important questions arising between employer and employed is that of the basis on which this payment is to be made. Broadly speaking, there are two possible bases of payment within the wage-system—payment for time worked and payment for output. There are indeed all kinds of modifications and minglings of these two principles; but they are none the less fundamentally distinct. A worker may be paid in strict accordance with the time spent on the employer's work at so much per hour, per day, per week, per month, or per year; or he or she may be paid in accordance with the work done at so much per piece, or per unit of effort. Again, the method of payment may be either individual or collective: the employer may deal separately with, and pay wages by time or output to, every worker individually, or a lump sum may be paid over to a single worker on behalf of a group, or to the group itself.

These two systems are, I have said, in principle distinct, however they may mingle in practice. But, to a very great extent, they do possess a common basis. A time-work system is never wholly without relation to output; for the employer inevitably expects a certain amount of work from the worker whom he employs, and if this amount is not forthcoming, he finds his remedy in discharging the worker. Payment by output, again, is never wholly without relation to a time standard; for piece-prices are invariably determined to a great extent by the income which constitutes the normal standard of life for the workmen concerned. This, however, is only to say that both time-workers and piece-workers are subject to the wage system.

This common basis of time payment and payment by output, however, does not remove their essential difference. Under a pure time-work system the employer no doubt expects and exacts a minimum standard of output; but the worker who produces less than this, as long as he continues to be employed, and the worker who produces more, both receive the same remuneration as the worker who produces exactly the minimum demanded. On a system of payment by output, on the other hand, the reference to a standard weekly wage may determine the general level of remuneration (*e.g.* the piece-work prices, bonuses, etc.); but the actual remuneration of the individual worker will vary with his or her output from day to day, or from week to week. Payment by time means equal payment to all workers who are classified together by the employer or by Trade Union regulation; payment by output means unequal remuneration for members of the same grade.

The difference between the two systems is well exemplified in the contest that has arisen concerning the principle of "equal pay for equal work" as between men and women. There is a dangerous ambiguity in this principle; for it does not say whether it means "equal pay for equal time" or "equal pay for equal output." Doubtless, the original meaning was that where women are employed on work previously done by men, they should be paid on the same system as the men and at the same rates, whether the payment were made by time or by output; but it has been argued—and the principle has been acted upon by the Government during the war—that "equal pay for equal work" means "equal pay for an equal amount of work done," *i.e.* for equal output, and that, where women produce less than men on time-work, they should accordingly receive a lower time-rate. This obviously strikes at the very basis of the time-work system, under which those workers who are doing the same kind of work all receive the same wage without regard to their output. At the same time it serves to drive home the point that a time-work system has necessarily some relation to the output expected of the worker.

This equality of remuneration between workers who are doing the same work is not, of course, inevitable under the time-work system. An employer might quite well, and to some extent does, differentiate between more and less capable workers even where payment is made by time. This differentiation, however, is sometimes checked by Trade Union action; for the Trade Union by collective bargaining aims at establishing a standard rate for each class of work; and it may, in some cases, be as impossible for the employer to pay more than the standard rate to an individual as for him to pay less. Were the employer dealing with all his workers individually, without the intervention of Trade Unions, differentiation would no doubt prevail widely in the case of time-workers; as things are, it happens most often when Trade Unionism is weak or non-existent. In other cases, particularly among salary-earners and employees of public bodies, a time-work system is combined with regular increments according to seniority.

A special modification of the time-work system, also destroying the uniformity of payment to men of the same trade, is in some cases sanctioned and even regularly arranged by the Trade Unions. This is where, within a craft, there are varying types of work in which the difference of capacity between workers is measurable less in terms of quantity, or output, than of quality of work. In such cases varying time-rates may exist according to the quality of the work to be done or according to the quality or grade of capacity of the worker. In the engineering industry a higher time-rate is often paid on work of special quality; and in the Furnishing Trades men are regularly rated according to capacity, as 1s. 3d. or 1s. an hour men. These modifications, however, do not alter the general principle of payment, which is still by time; for any two workers who are rated at the same figure will receive the same remuneration without regard to the actual output secured and, in the last case, equally without regard to the actual quality of the work done.

We have seen that time-work has, in practically all cases, some reference to output, in that the employer can and does dismiss a man who is not doing what he regards as a fair, or an average, day's work. This principle, however, is very elastically applied, and under an ordinary time-work system it is seldom possible to say exactly what is the minimum amount of work required by the employer. Where the minimum becomes fixed, time-work passes over into task-work. The task-work system, in its complete form, is a system under which the worker is set a definite output which must be attained per day, or per week, or per month. If the fixed output is not attained, a proportionate deduction is made from the wages paid to the worker; if it is exceeded, nothing extra is paid. Needless to say, this system is strenuously opposed by the workers, nor does it exist in any organised trade; but many of the features of the task-work system exist in those cases in which a certain output is rigidly exacted, and the worker who fails to reach that output is at once dismissed. In these cases there is no deduction from wages for failure to produce the standard amount; but in certain trades the threat of summary dismissal has even more effect in securing the imposition of a "task" than could ever be exercised by deductions from wages. Task-work is a variant of time-work in that the payment made is proportionate not to output, but to time spent; but in it the common basis of the two systems appears in the clearest form, since a minimum output is the condition of receiving the time-wage.

Not a few of the "efficiency" systems which are connected with the name of "Scientific Management" reproduce some of the conditions of task-work in that they penalise by a specially low rate of payment the worker who fails to reach a certain standard of output, and reward the worker who reaches or exceeds this output. These systems of rewards and penalties applied by an unscrupulous employer to badly organised workers may be fully as objectionable as a task-work system.

Systems of payment by output are far more various and complicated than time-work systems. In some cases payment by output is the natural and almost inevitable remuneration for certain kinds of service which cannot easily be paid by time: in others it is a conscious device for the acceleration of production. In the first case the system tends to be simple; in the second the employer, in a continual search for new stimuli, tends to adopt more and more complicated devices, and very often a job passes through successive stages of time-payment, piece-payment, and bonus or "reward" payment. The principle of ordinary piece-work is essentially simple. Instead of receiving so much per hour, the worker receives so much for every operation, or group of operations, performed, at a flat rate per operation, the wages received being strictly proportionate to output. There are, however, many modifications of this system in practice. Where Trade Unions are strong, they generally attempt to secure a guarantee that the earnings of the piece-worker will not fall below the hourly rate of wages. Not only do the Unions seek to establish piece-prices on such a basis that actual earnings under piece-work conditions shall be above the standard time-rate; they also demand an absolute guarantee that every worker shall receive at least the standard time-rate, without reference to output. In some few cases they have gone further, and have provided that, since piece-work is openly advocated on the ground that it secures greater output and therefore greater effort from the worker, more than the standard time-rate (*e.g.* time and a quarter) shall be guaranteed to every individual who is working on piece-work. These systems alike serve to emphasise the time-work basis on which piece-work usually rests; and, in practice, piece-work prices are usually regarded as fair if they yield about a certain percentage settled by custom above the time-rate to the average worker.

Naturally, piece-work is most easily adaptable to those occupations in which the work done is "repetition" work, *i.e.* in which an identical job is repeated an indefinite number of times. This is the position in all manufacturing industries which are highly standardised, and especially in the textile industries. It does not matter in such cases whether the number of distinct jobs is large or small; for provided that they are repetitive in character, a standard price can be fixed for each job. Where the number of jobs is small and their nature simple, piece-work conditions are easily adjusted: when jobs are numerous and complicated, the most elaborate systems are sometimes adopted for the fixing and maintenance of piece-work prices.

In such cases, the Trade Union finds its natural function in establishing the principle of collective bargaining in relation to piece-work prices, and the method adopted in the great repetitive industries where Trade Unionism is strong has been that of the standard price list—a long list, usually printed and sometimes of quite extraordinary complexity, setting forth in full the piece-work price to be paid for every job regularly executed in the industry. Such lists are sometimes established for a particular works, and sometimes arrived at by agreement between the Unions and the employers for the whole industry, or for a whole district, subject in many cases to modifications to meet the conditions in particular works.

Piece-work, however, is by no means confined to jobs of a repetitive character. It is often applied to trades and in cases in which a standard price list cannot be automatically applied to a series of identical jobs. In these cases the principle of collective bargaining is by no means so easy to enforce; and in some skilled trades its place has hitherto been taken by what is called "mutuality," *i.e.* the fixing of a piece-price for an individual job by mutual agreement between the employer, acting through his representative, and the workman or workmen who perform the job. Where this occurs, individual mutuality has often a measure of collective backing; for the men in the shop naturally act together in the adjustment of piece-prices, either through an organised committee or by unorganised co-operation. Thus piece-work prices become to some extent fixed by workshop custom; but even so there is usually no approach to the fixity and almost automatic operation of the standard price list. One of the main questions with which we shall have to deal in this book is that of the relative spheres of the standard list and of "mutuality," and in this connection we shall treat more fully of the methods by which the collective backing of "mutuality" can be most effectively strengthened. Here it is only necessary to say that "mutuality" operates very differently in the case of skilled workers who are well organised and trained to co-operation, and in that of less skilled workers who are badly organised and lack such training. This applies with special force in the case of women piece-workers.

Naturally, the standard price list has reached its most perfect form in those trades which are most highly standardised, especially in the cotton trades. "Mutuality," on the other hand, is most prevalent where the jobs are not so repetitive in character, or where the machinery on which the job is to be done is not of a standard pattern. The chief instance of the second type has been the engineering industry, though here the standardisation of recent years, and still more of the war period, has introduced many changes, and in some cases has no doubt rendered "mutuality" in effect obsolete.

So far we have been speaking of piece-work as a uniform system of payment strictly in proportion to output. It now remains to mention some of the variations of this general principle. Cases exist, though they are not frequent, in which, under a straight piece-work system, the piece-price diminishes as output increases, the price per article diminishing after the output has reached a certain point. On the other hand, in some cases the piece-price increases with increased output, in order that production may be stimulated to the full. This motive, however, more generally expresses itself in the granting of a bonus after output has passed a given point. Thus, at this stage, the piece-work system develops into the bonus system. It is, however, paradoxically true that most bonus systems actually effect a reduction in the price per piece as the output increases.

Bonuses, as an incentive to output, take several forms. The simplest is that which we have just described, the bonus being merely superimposed upon the piece-work system without any essential change in the method of remuneration. In other cases a bonus of the same type is superimposed upon a time-work system. Only in the premium bonus system and in some American " efficiency " systems does a really distinct form of payment arise. In the various forms of the premium bonus system the basis is no longer a piece-price per article, but a standard time allowance in which the job is supposed to be done. If time is saved by the worker, that is, if the job is done at greater speed and in a time less than the standard allowance, payment is made for a portion of the time saved in addition to the hours actually worked. Thus in the simplest form known as the Halsey system, if the standard time allowance for a job is ten hours, and the worker does the job in six hours, payment will be made for six hours, and in addition for a proportion, very often a half, of the four hours saved in the job. This payment will be made at the standard hourly rate. Thus the premium bonus system takes as its basis the standard time-rate, which is practically always guaranteed to every worker under the system. Everything, of course, depends upon the standard time allowance fixed for the job. If this is high, the worker will be able to save a considerable time, and so to earn high wages ; if it is low, only the hourly rate or a very little more may be earned. In fact, exactly the same problems present themselves in the fixing of standard time allowances under the premium bonus system as in the fixing of piece-work prices, and exactly the same arguments about price lists and " mutuality " apply. Hitherto, however, the premium bonus system has been practically confined to trades in which the standard price list is non-existent, and standard time allowances have been fixed by " mutuality " where Trade Unionism is strong, and by the arbitrary imposition of the employer where it is weak or non-existent.

There is one other method of remuneration which deserves a mention side by side with those described above. This is profit-sharing in its various forms. We have seen that the employer often desires to adopt a system of payment by results as an incentive to output. This end he may strive to attain in another way by giving his employees an "interest in the business." Instead of affording them a chance of earning time and a quarter or even time and a half on piece-work or the premium bonus system, he may pay them a percentage on wages varying with the profits of the concern. This is, of course, quite different in principle, though those employers who advocate it have the same end in view—and perhaps other ends as well. It is, however, a distinct method of payment, and one which has been, and may yet be, advocated as an alternative to piece-work or the premium bonus system; and the fact that it may be put forward as an alternative entitles it to a place in our consideration.

In this brief introduction I have tried to give a very general summary of the main types of wage-payment without entering at all into their relative merits as methods of operating the wage system. Criticism and assessment of values will be easier when we have gone into more detail, and examined the operation of the various systems in some of the principal industries. The treatment adopted in the main portion of this book is that of dealing with the problems of wage-payment one by one, those cases being selected which serve to bring out the main principles. In the later chapters the reader will find an attempt not only at criticism of existing methods, but also at a constructive policy for Trade Unionism in the immediate future. The controversy about methods of payment is one which, in some trade or other, is always acute. It is a permanent source of trouble in the engineering trades. In the building trades, it crops up from time to time when some group of employers attempts to impose " payment by results " upon crafts traditionally associated with time-work. Outside the textile industries, there is scarcely a trade that is free from it; even in the mines it looms in the background as a constant source of friction. In dealing with this problem, it is important that Trade Unionists should be equipped with knowledge, not only about their own trades, but also about industry generally; for in many cases it will be found that the same problems occur in different industries, and that one trade has made some approach to a solution where another has lagged behind. The main object of this book is to bring clearly into light the principles underlying the whole question.

CHAPTER II

THE POSITION IN CERTAIN INDUSTRIES

How does it come about that workers are paid in some jobs according to the time spent in the employer's service, and in others according to the work done or output secured? What are, in practice, the main factors which decide whether a job shall be paid for on time-rates, or on one of the many systems of "payment by results"? There is, indeed, no absolute logic in the matter; but even a superficial examination of the practice prevailing in various trades serves to show some at least of the main reasons for adopting the one system or the other.

I shall be able to bring these reasons most clearly before the reader's mind if I undertake a rapid survey of the methods of payment in some of the principal trades and industries. This is the purpose of the present chapter.

In their standard work on Trade Union problems and policy published more than twenty years ago,[1] Mr. and Mrs. Sidney Webb included a table designed to illustrate the attitude of the various Trade Unions at that time to systems of payment by results.[2] The net result of their investigations was briefly this. Omitting from their survey the transport and general labour Unions, they found 42 Trade Unions, with a total membership of 573,000, which insisted upon piece-work, 38 Trade Unions, with a membership of 290,000, which insisted on time-work, and 24 Unions, with 140,000 members, which recognised both methods of payment.

It may be doubted whether this calculation was ever of any high degree of accuracy, and it would certainly not be possible to make an accurate estimate on the same basis to-day; for now, to a greater extent than twenty years ago, very diverse types of workers are included in the same Trade Unions, with the result that, a few prominent exceptions apart, most Unions include both time-workers and piece-workers. We cannot, then, at the present time present any numerical estimate of the proportion of piece-workers in industry, or of the attitude of Trade Unions to systems of pay-

[1] In 1897.

[2] See *Industrial Democracy*, pp. 286-7.

ment by results. It is only possible to define the attitude of the main groups of workers and to describe the systems under which they actually work.

The tendency of the last two decades has undoubtedly been in the direction of a more widespread adoption of payment by results. This tendency has been furthered by the rapid development of machinery, and of fixed capital generally, which has reduced the proportion which labour cost bears to the total cost of production, and it has been greatly accelerated in some industries by the war. It is, however, doubtful whether, outside the engineering and allied industries, there has been any very great change in the relative number of piece-workers and day-workers.

In most manufacturing industries, though not in all, the Trade Unions, at any rate nationally, do not to-day so much insist on either day-work or payment by results as endeavour to lay down the conditions under which either system may be worked. The textile industries are still almost entirely piece-work industries: the building industry, on the other hand, maintains unaltered its firm opposition to all systems of payment by results. But in other cases the tendency is for systems of payment by results to encroach gradually upon time-work systems, sometimes in face of more or less determined Trade Union opposition.

With this brief introduction, we may proceed at once to our survey of the field of industry. Perforce, we shall ignore all but the main groups; but those that are dealt with furnish a fair sample of the whole.

I. Let us begin with the transport industries, which Mr. and Mrs. Webb omitted from their survey. Railway work is, of course, owing to its nature, almost all day-work, if we except construction work in the locomotive shops, which comes under the heading of engineering. There are in some railways "mileage" bonuses for locomotive drivers, and piece-work in goods yards is not unknown on certain work; but these are almost insignificant exceptions to the general rule—unless, indeed, the variable "tips" of railway porters are to be regarded as instances of "payment by results."

Other forms of land transport work again, whether on tram, bus, lorry, or cart, are almost necessarily time-work. The exception is the taxi-driver, who is in effect a piece-worker of a peculiar type.

Waterside work admits of both systems. Coal trimming and bunkering is almost always piece-work. It calls for very great strength and for the utmost exertion, and therefore an incentive is, under present conditions, necessary to secure its execution. It is, moreover, work at which no man is strong enough to work regularly six days a week; and the workers prefer a piece-work system, not only because it secures them higher earnings, but also because it leaves them freer in their comings and goings. In normal times the worker in this occupation goes "all out" for a few days, and then rests for a few days: and this would be very difficult under a time-work system.

The loading and unloading of other standard products such as iron ore, grain, pit props and other timber, and anything else easily calculable in terms of weight or measurement, is often done on piece-work, at so much per ton, per sack, etc., with elaborate special tariffs to meet special cases. This, however, is not universal, and the custom varies from port to port for no ascertainable reason. In some ports (*e.g.* Liverpool) there has been in recent years a tendency on the men's side to endeavour to eliminate piece-work altogether; in others (*e.g.* Newport) attempts by the employers to introduce time-work have been strenuously resisted by the men.

Work at sea, whether it be that of the sailors, the cooks and stewards, or the marine engineers, is again necessarily time-work.

II. We may deal next with the group of extractive industries. Mining is, in the main, a piece-work industry. In all districts the vast majority of the actual coal-getters or hewers are paid by the ton. Underground haulage is usually, but not always, paid for in the same way. But, with regard to other classes of colliery labour, there is very great variety in the customs of different districts. In South Wales every possible type of work is on a piece-work basis, even surface haulage being paid for on a collective tonnage rate. In other districts, as in Durham, the greater part of the work, other than actual coal-getting, is paid for on day-work rates. At the Annual Conference of the Miners' Federation of Great Britain in 1916, the Lancashire and Cheshire delegates brought forward a resolution in favour of the entire abolition of piece-work, largely on the ground that it would reduce the danger of accidents. This has been described as "a feeler resolution"; but there is no doubt that it has received considerable support.

Agriculture is in the main a time-work industry, and could, for the most part, not be anything else, although harvesting, and to a less extent certain other operations, are often done wholly or partly on a piece-work basis.

III. We come now to the group of metal industries, beginning with the processes of manufacturing iron and steel from the ore and of producing plates, rails, tin-plates, etc. So far as "direct" workers are concerned, the iron and steel industry is almost entirely a piece-work industry, though there are large numbers of "additional" workers, mechanics, enginemen, labourers, etc., who are paid by time. The product is in these cases standardised, and lends itself easily to the computation of wages in terms of output on a tonnage basis. The standard price list therefore prevails.

Foundry work cannot be so easily classified. Loose-box moulding in connection with engineering works or in jobbing or contract foundries, in which the bulk of the heavy and the most skilful work is done, is mainly paid on a day-work basis, though there are a number of shops in which piece-work, and even bonus, systems exist. The two principal Unions catering for this class of worker, the Friendly Society of Ironfounders and the Associated Iron-moulders of Scotland, while they are not prepared to take drastic action to abolish piece-work where it has become established, oppose its extension and abolish it where they can.

The less skilled and more repetitive moulding work connected with the light casting trade, especially the manufacture of stoves, grates, fenders, baths, etc., lends itself more easily to piece-work methods, including the listing of prices, and is more often remunerated on a piece-work basis.

Machine-moulding, especially in textile and agricultural machinery and railway shops, is largely piece-work.

There are, of course, in all classes of foundries, large numbers of workers other than moulders who are mainly paid by time. Core-making, however, is often done on a piece-work system, and in some districts the foreman is in the position of a sub-contractor.

Patternmaking is almost entirely time-work, and the Unions concerned do not admit any other system, though in a few cases the employers have succeeded in introducing bonus systems. In their opposition to payment by results the patternmakers resemble practically the whole of the woodworking trades.

Turning now to general engineering, we find an industry far more diversified, and one in which the two systems exist side by side. Repetition workers and semi-skilled machine workers are very often paid by the piece; the methods of paying skilled workers vary, not only with the character of the work done, but also with district and workshop custom. The engineering Trade Unions long refused to recognise any piece-work system; but at the close of the 1897 strike they were compelled to accept the employers' right to introduce payment by results, and this acceptance was continued in the subsequent agreements of 1901 and 1907, while the Premium Bonus Memorandum signed at Carlisle in 1902 extended the acceptance to that system also in the case of the Amalgamated Society of Engineers, the chief Union in the industry. The Amalgamated Society of Engineers, however, terminated the 1907 agreement by notice in 1914, just before the outbreak of the war; but the war has prevented any new adjustment from being made.

The effect of the war has been to bring about, under Government pressure, a big increase in payment by results; but this has been strongly objected to by the Unions, and they have refused, even during the war, any general acceptance of the system. One of the main objections to payment by results in the engineering industry lies in the complete absence of any systematic regulation of piece-work prices or bonus times, and the very great practical difficulty of applying in such cases the method of collective bargaining.

Blacksmithing is in much the same position as other engineering work. Piece-work and bonus systems are disliked by the Unions;

but in a good many cases the employers have secured their adoption.

Shipyard work is largely piece-work. The largest Union, the Boilermakers, consists largely of piece-workers, and has elaborate methods of regulating piece-work prices by collective bargaining. Shipwrights' work was, before the war, time-work; but piece-work has been introduced during the war. This applies to some other shipyard crafts. Drillers, who are organised in a separate section of the Shipwrights' Society, are piece-workers who work mostly under standard price lists. Most woodworking crafts, however, insist on time-work even in the shipyards; and this applies also to the plumbers, painters, and other crafts. There has been a big increase during the war in the payment of shipyard work by results, and the Admiralty has conducted a special campaign with this object in view. Marine engineering is in much the same position as general engineering.

Sheet-metal work is partly time-work and partly piece-work. The Midland makers of domestic utensils, tin boxes, etc., are mostly piece-workers, while most of the shipyard sheet-metal workers remain under a time-work system.

The miscellaneous metal trades are too various to admit of clear classification; but the greater number of those employed are piece-workers. In some cases, as in the brass trades, special systems are in force, the "grading scheme" of the Birmingham brassworkers being of special interest and importance.

The woodworking trades—carpenters and joiners, cabinet-makers, furnishing trades, upholsterers, coachmakers and wheelwrights, as well as patternmakers—are almost entirely time-work trades, at all events wherever effective Trade Unions exist. The Unions regard payment by results as utterly unsuited to the conditions of their work, and many disputes have arisen, both before and during the war, out of attempts to introduce such systems.

The building industry is the great example of a time-work industry in which acute controversy has existed concerning the proper method of wage-payment. The building trades—stonemasons, bricklayers, plasterers, slaters and tilers, plumbers and heating engineers, painters and the various woodworking crafts mentioned above, as well as scaffolders and other builders' labourers—all insist on day-work rates.

The printing industry admits both systems; but it is mainly a day-work industry. Compositors in London, including both case hands and machine operators, work both on time-work and on piece-work, governed by a comprehensive list of prices, but, in practice, except on newspaper work, time-work largely preponderates. In the provinces time-work is even more general, although the Typographical Association recognises piece-work on linotype and monotype machines. The other crafts are mainly time-workers; but bookbinding is a mixed trade in which the two systems exist side by side.

The great textile industries are the natural home of piece-work systems. Their products are, in most cases, dependent on power-driven machinery, the speed of which is dictated by the employer. They are, moreover, absolutely standardised, and admit of ready calculation in terms of output. Elaborate price lists agreed between Employers' Associations and Trade Unions are therefore the rule, and provide for most contingencies. These have been brought to the greatest perfection in the cotton industry of Lancashire, but they exist in the woollen and other textile industries as well, though they are far less complete and show far less uniformity from district to district. Disputes in these trades arise mainly from employers' complaints as to faulty work and workmen's complaints as to defective material.

The clothing trades work under various systems, piece-work being almost universal where large-scale factory production exists, while the two systems exist side by side in the smaller workshops. Some of the worst "sweat-shops" are time-work establishments, in which supervision and over-drive are used to maintain output in preference to the incentive of a piece-work rate. The sweated home-workers are, of course, always paid by the piece.

The boot and shoe industry recognises both systems; but piece-work has long been gaining ground at the expense of time-work, and the war has greatly hastened this process. The product being standardised, piece-work prices can be readily calculated; and elaborate lists of prices exist. It is interesting to notice that the National Union of Boot and Shoe Operatives insists that, where piece-work is introduced into any shop or department, its introduction shall be universal. The two systems are never allowed to be worked side by side in the same department.

The glass and pottery trades work mainly under piece-work systems, very imperfectly safeguarded as a rule by collective bargaining, although in some cases workshop committees exist and secure recognition. The more skilled workers in the pottery trades especially tend to prefer piece-work because they hold that it gives them greater freedom as to time-keeping. This is, no doubt, largely due to the continuance of small-scale production in the industry.

Of the many smaller manufacturing industries I can only speak generally. As these smaller industries are less organised on both sides, there is naturally less uniformity of practice than in cases where Trade Unionism is strong among employers and workers alike. What has been said of tailoring and clothing generally applies to many other weakly organised industries. Time-work is often found where wages are lowest and sweating most prevalent, because where the workers are weak it is possible for the employers to exact piece-work intensity for a time rate of wages. It would, however, be a mistake to generalise on this point. The worst "sweater" may adopt either time-work or piece-work as a method of payment, and his actual choice depends as much on accident or custom as on the fitness of the trade concerned for the one system or the other.

The distributive trades, wholesale and retail, co-operative and private, are naturally in the main time-work trades, though systems of part payment in commission on takings are unpleasantly prevalent in some branches of retail trade. In some cases these commission systems apply only to managers: in others the private trader puts practically his whole staff on commission. This practice is naturally resisted by the Trade Unions, and could not persist if the distributive trades were fully organised. It may be added that various subsidiary processes connected with distribution, such as bottling, packing, labelling, etc., are largely done under piece-work conditions.

Clerical work of all sorts, whether the employer be the Government, a local authority, an office, or a railway company, is almost necessarily time-work, though here, too, in some cases a commission system creeps in on commercial work. It may be mentioned in this connection that some of the most sweated classes of workers, such as envelope addressers, work by the piece. Full-time typists are employed at weekly rates; but the independent typist usually gains a precarious livelihood at so much per thousand words.

The Post Office is an example of a time-work industry with an elaborate system of remuneration based upon graded incremental scales of salaries and wages.

We may now perhaps sum up by way of a table the various facts of which we have given a rapid survey. This table cannot be exact, because in most industries time-work and payment by results exist side by side. All we can do is to give a general impression of the prevalent system of payment in each of the principal industrial groups.

A. *Industries in which the nature of the work usually necessitates payment by time.*

Transport Group. { Railways.
Tramways and Omnibus Services.
Carting.
Work on board ship. }

Agriculture.
Distribution.
Clerical Work.

B. *Industries other than those in Group A in which time-work is actually the prevailing system.*

Building and Woodworking.
Printing.

C. *Industries in which systems of payment by results prevail.*

Mining.
Iron and Steel and Tinplate.
Textiles.
Pottery and Glass.

D. *Industries in which both systems exist.*

Waterside Work.
Engineering and Foundry Work.
Shipyards.
Miscellaneous Metal Trades.
Clothing.
Boot and Shoe.

It should be said that in Group D the Trade Union attitude to piece-work varies very widely, not only as between industry and industry, but also as between craft and craft.

We can now pass to a more definite attempt to estimate the causes which make for the adoption of the one method of payment in preference to the other. Custom, of course, plays a big part in most cases; but custom, though sometimes irrational, is often the product of long experience. Where the one method or the other is in general operation, it is fairly clear that either employers or workmen, or both, have some reason for regarding it as the best system for their trade.

The causes leading to the adoption of payment by results are various. We hear most nowadays in this connection of the need for increasing output and making the most of our industrial plant; and, from the manufacturer's point of view, this need becomes increasingly urgent as the machinery used becomes more complicated and more expensive. This, however, has not been in the past by any means the only cause. To the economic individualist, the only just system of remuneration seems to be one which rewards each individual worker according to the amount of work done by him. The Trade Union standard rate is continually attacked by employers and economists on the ground that it tends to ensure the same remuneration to the less capable and to the "slacker" as to the more capable or more energetic workers. This argument has not been without its force among Trade Union leaders of the individualist school. For instance, it was strongly emphasised by Mr. W. J. Davis, General Secretary of the National Society of Brassworkers, when he was arguing in favour of the scheme—now in force in the Birmingham brass trade—of grading workers according to capacity. In this case, indeed, the alternatives put forward were not time-work and piece-work, but a flat standard rate and graded standard rates for workers of varying capacity; but the principle involved in the argument was the same. As long as payment is made for work done, as it is under all existing systems of industrial organisation, there will clearly be a tendency among individualists to regard payment by results as the most equitable system.

These, however, are in the main the arguments of employers and economists of the employing class. Let us see, if we can, what are the reasons that have led the workers in a number of trades and industries to prefer payment by results. The individualist argument, as we have seen, counts in this case also; but it would be easy to overestimate its importance in the workman's eyes. The arguments which he uses in favour of payment by results are usually quite different. In the first place, in a number of trades the workmen claim that payment by results leaves them more their own masters. They are more free to take time off from their work, less tied to continuous application, and less subject to continuous supervision and overdrive by foremen and managers. This argument is of very varying importance in different classes of work. To the coal-trimmer, whose work is discontinuous, and to many craftsmen who work in small shops and are more or less on an equality with their employers, it is of the greatest weight; to workers in highly organised industries and under large-scale production it applies in a far less degree.

Secondly, payment by results does mean, in many cases, an increase in earnings, at least over a limited period, and, for the wage-earner of to-day, an increase in earnings means a rather better chance of living the sort of life which all reasonable beings ought to be in a position to live. Payment by results does undoubtedly, in a number of trades, increase output, and therewith earnings, even if, in some cases, the effect on the standard rate is, in the long run, unfavourable.

On the other hand, in some cases payment by results is opposed by employers and workers on other grounds. Again, the reasons are various. The employer may hold that he can get better results out of his workers by paying more for supervision and driving them hard than by increasing his direct wages bill. In short, he may hope to get, and in some cases may actually get, piece-work intensity for time wages. This is usually the position, for instance, of the sub-contractor, "piece-master" or "butty-man." He may further have a conviction that it is almost immoral for his workers' earnings to rise above a certain level; but this is even more likely to lead to piece-work combined with price-cutting than to a time-work system. Thirdly, the employer may have a better motive. Quality may count for much in his work, and he may hold that the adoption of payment by results will lead to a deterioration in the quality of the product.

The worker's objections to payment by results are more complex. In the first place, he fears speeding-up beyond what he regards as "a fair day's work." Secondly, he fears that speeding-up will be used for the purpose of reducing prices, and that, if he produces more, his employer will cut rates and secure the benefit in extra profits. Thirdly, he is proud of his craftsmanship, and fears that payment by results will have a bad effect on the quality of the product. Fourthly, he fears that an increased product per man per hour will mean less employment for himself and his fellows, and increased liability to unemployment, with all that unemployment entails. Fifthly, he sees that the effect of payment by results is in many cases to set man against man, and that, whereas time-work and the standard rate conduce to solidarity, payment by results makes workmen jealous and suspicious one of another.

These human reasons for and against payment by results are of very different importance under different circumstances, and we shall return to them all in subsequent chapters. Here we are only concerned to state opinions without analysing their real value.

To these human considerations many others must be added. We have seen that some branches of industry must necessarily be conducted under a system of payment for time worked, and that these include nearly all clerical work and the bulk of transport work. It is not the case that there are any trades or industries in which payment by results is the only possible system, unless work done in the worker's home be so regarded; but it is the case that some industries, by their very nature, lend themselves easily to such a method of remuneration.

As we saw in the first chapter, one of the main determining factors under any system of payment by results is the degree in which a given amount of effort or skill can be relied upon to produce a given result. This is naturally the case roughly in proportion as the products, the processes, and the machinery used are standardised. A worker producing a standard product by a standard process on a standard machine will differ in productivity from another worker on the same job according to the effort used, and the skill or dexterity with which that effort is applied. Payment according to production, therefore, will in such a case mean payment according to the productive value of the worker, and will therefore so far conform to the individualist standard of justice. Of course it is never possible to eliminate entirely conditions affecting production which are outside the worker's control; but these factors may be relatively unimportant, and may be held to average out fairly over a reasonably long period. Where they cannot be relied on to "average out," they are sometimes compensated for by special allowances of various kinds. This is the position in the cotton industry, and, to a less extent, in many other kinds of repetition work, and this is enough to account for the prevalence, in such cases, of payment by results.

Even where the material factors are less uniform, but the product is absolutely a standard product, readily measurable in quantitative terms, there will be a strong tendency to adopt payment by results; for here, too, favouritism or ill-luck, apart from good and bad conditions, will be likely to "average out" fairly over a period of time. This is the position with regard to coal-getting, and the production of manufactured iron and steel. The balance between earnings and effort and skill is less accurate; but, in the bulk of cases, the worker is paid according to his productive value. This individualist justice is not by any means absolute. In the coal mines, for instance, the peculiar difficulty of the "abnormal place" has to be specially provided for; but such difficulties are none the less in the nature of exceptions.

Thirdly, where there is not even this rough accuracy, and where the product is not so readily measurable in purely quantitative terms, the conditions may be such as to encourage the adoption of payment by results. If the overhead charges or "oncost" of an industrial process are very high, and a considerable saving can be effected by getting a bigger production from the machine, it may pay the employer to offer what seem to be generous terms in order to secure greater production. This is undoubtedly the case in certain manufacturing processes, notably in engineering and shipbuilding, where the workers are too strongly organised to be speeded-up by any method other than that of extra inducements.

Fourthly, even where none of the above conditions is present in a high degree, the continuance of a system of payment by results may be made easy by the existence of a well-organised system of collective bargaining about piece-work prices or basis-time allowances, under which the difficulties and abnormalities arising under the system are constantly corrected and adjusted by organised effort on both sides. This is, I think, the position of the boilermakers, drillers, and certain of the smaller metal trades, as well as of the piece-working compositors.

It is clear that, even in industries in which some of the above conditions exist, the workmen's objection to piece-work is upheld largely by the absence of any satisfactory method of safeguarding piece-work prices. An unregulated system of payment by results, under which the employer or his foremen fix and readjust prices for successive jobs at their own sweet will, is certainly the worst possible system of payment for all except the few most rapid and dexterous workers. Employers would probably have encountered far less resistance to their efforts to establish payment by results had they not so often attempted to introduce it in this form, and thus to use it as a method of defeating collective bargaining.

We may now sum up briefly the results of this chapter. We have seen that a system of payment by results is easiest to establish and operate where the following conditions are present:

(1) Where a given amount of effort and skill can be relied upon to result in a given product.

(2) Where the product is easily measurable in simple quantitative terms (*e.g.* by the ton).

(3) Where increased productivity means a considerable saving in standing charges, and thereby a reduction in the cost of production per unit.
(4) Where a highly developed system of collective bargaining exists, or where such a system can be created.

We have seen further what are the main inducements for the employer to press for payment by results:

(1) The desire for increased output as a means of reducing the cost of production (this is the same as (3) above).
(2) The feeling that individualist justice will be done if each worker is rewarded according to his productive efficiency.
(3) In some cases, the possibility of ascertaining the amount the worker is capable of producing, and then of cutting prices to the lowest possible limit.

Next we saw the worker's reasons for preferring payment by results in certain cases:

(1) The possibility of greater freedom in respect of time-keeping and attention to work.
(2) The chance of higher earnings, and the greater interest given to the work by the monetary inducement.
(3) In some cases, the same individualist feeling as we ascribed to the employers.

We then turned to the arguments on the other side, and first we dealt with these from the employer's point of view:

(1) The possibility of cheapening cost by supervision and drive, and of securing piece-work intensity for time-rates of wages.
(2) In some cases, the feeling that it is immoral for the workman to earn more than his standard rate.
(3) In some cases, the desire to preserve a high quality of workmanship.

Lastly, we saw the working-class objections:

(1) The fear of speeding-up.
(2) The fear of price-cutting following on speeding-up.
(3) The desire to preserve a high standard of craftsmanship.
(4) The fear of unemployment due to a higher productivity per man in an inelastic market.
(5) The fear that payment by results will break up solidarity by setting man against man and breeding mutual jealousy and suspicion.

In this chapter I have set good and bad, real and true, reasons down together without attempting any valuation of them. I have done this because it is important at the outset to understand the different points of view of the various sections of workers and employers, in order that we may be able to approach the problem of wage-payment from a human, as well as from a purely industrial, standpoint. These facts clear in our minds, we can proceed to discuss the various problems with a far better grasp of the general situation.

CHAPTER III

OUTPUT

THE argument usually adduced by the employer who desires to introduce some system of payment by results is the necessity of increasing output. The workman, he contends, cannot be persuaded, under a time-work system, to turn out a "fair day's work": he needs some stimulus, some incentive of immediate personal gain, before he can be induced to put out his full effort. Payment by results, it is said, provides this stimulus, and secures at the same time higher earnings for the workman and a lower cost of production for the employer. Both employer and workman benefit, and—so the argument runs—the national industry benefits also.

In support of this contention employers are fond of drawing comparisons between British industry and German or American industry. Output, they tell us, is far higher in the United States and in Germany, where systems of payment by results obtain to a greater extent than in this country. These parallels are drawn very largely from the engineering industry; but it is interesting to note that American Trade Unionist mechanics have, on the whole, shown themselves even more hostile to payment by results than those of Great Britain. If payment by results means a paradise for workman as well as for employer it seems curious that this should be the case.

In fact, comparisons with foreign countries based on statistics of output are liable to be completely misleading. They take, for the most part, no account of the character of the product or of the conditions under which production is carried on. As a result, many of the recent attempts to institute payment by results in this country have been attempts to graft conditions applicable only to standardised methods of production on to methods which are the very reverse of standardised.

However this country may compare with others in respect of restriction of output, there can be no doubt that, in the majority of cases, the introduction of payment by results is followed by an immediate increase in output. The incentive afforded by a piecework or bonus system does get more out of the worker, at least until he has become accustomed to it, and out of some workers it will always get more.

It would, however, be the greatest possible mistake to suppose that the practices which the employers and the newspapers call "restriction of output" obtain only under time-work conditions. This is, in fact, the very opposite of the truth. Many of the most bitter and continual complaints about restriction of output have been made by employers in trades in which payment by results actually obtains, and piece-workers and premium bonus-workers have come in for more than their share of the blame. I do not mean to suggest that payment by results necessarily leads to restriction of output, but I do suggest that it very often does so, especially where it is applied to non-standardised trades, or without being accompanied by a complete system of collective bargaining.

Before we go further we must endeavour to explain this phenomenon which is known as "restriction of output." The phrase is very loosely used, and is made to bear a variety of meanings, of which at least four can be definitely stated.

(1) "Restriction of output" is most naturally used in the sense of deliberate *ca' canny*, which means going slowly on purpose, usually with a definite object in view. This practice ranges from the temporary adoption of the "stay-in strike," as a method of getting redress for a particular grievance, to continual limitation of output, often on a particular job, for the purpose of keeping up piece-work prices or basis-time allowances.

(2) The second sense attached to the phrase relates it closely to the conception of a "fair day's work." As long as employers and employed exist, there are likely to be two views as to the amount of energy that constitutes a "fair day's work." The employer will have one view, and the workman another; and the former will accuse the latter of "restriction of output" if he fails to put out the higher standard of effort.

(3) The phrase "restriction of output" is commonly extended to many questions besides the amount of effort exerted by the individual workman. Trade Unions or workmen lay down in many cases elaborate regulations with regard to the type of workman who is to be allowed to do a particular job or to operate a particular class of machine. Such regulations are often denounced as restrictive of output on the ground that they prevent the employer from making the fullest possible use of the labour power at his command.

(4) Similar accusations are made against other working rules laid down by Trade Unions or enforced by concert among the men in a particular shop. It is applied particularly to rules limiting overtime or regulating the supply and distribution of work in the workshop, or imposing prohibitions or restrictions on the working of systems of payment by results.

There are, no doubt, many other senses sometimes attached to the phrase "restriction of output." Those enumerated above seem, however, to be the commonest and the most easily defined, and if we concentrate upon them, we shall be covering most of the ground that is in dispute.

We must next note that there are at least four ways in which collective "restriction of output," in the senses defined above, can take place.

(1) The "restriction" may be definitely imposed by the rules of a Trade Union. Instances of this are the definite prohibition of piece-work, and bonus systems, which is found in the rule-books of some Trade Unions (Carpenters and Joiners, etc.), and the far more frequent rules prohibiting the introduction of piece-work or bonus systems into any shop in which it is not already established and urging its abolition where it exists (Stonemasons, Heating Engineers, Iron, Steel, and Brass Dressers, Coremakers, Ironfounders, Blacksmiths, Electrical Trades Union, etc.), or restricting its operation by elaborate conditions (Amalgamated Society of Engineers, Coppersmiths, Boilermakers, Coachmakers, etc.).

(2) The "restriction" may be imposed, not by rule, but by local bye-laws of a Trade Union. Thus many of the above Trade Unions have more detailed regulations governing the operation of payment by results in particular districts, or regulating overtime or the class of labour to be employed on particular machines.

(3) The "restriction" may form part of a collective agreement signed and accepted by the employers, either locally or nationally. Such agreements usually arise out of trade disputes or are brought into being with a view to the prevention of disputes. Instances are the various engineering agreements. the Typographical Association's agreements with regard to piece-work on monotype and linotype machines, the Glasgow Furnishing Trades Piece-work Agreement, and many others.

(4) The "restriction" may be an unwritten custom of a workshop, district, or trade, nowhere expressly stated, but usually adhered to by all the workmen. Instances are naturally harder to give; but employers continually denounce the existence of such compacts. Restriction of entry to the trade, restriction on the employment of non-union labour or of workers not belonging to the particular Union imposing the restriction, and concerted limitation of the amount of work done are the practices most frequently denounced under this head.

Let us now try to compare these four ways of imposing restrictions with the four main types of restriction imposed.

(1) Ca' canny, or deliberate going slow, is not countenanced in any Trade Union rule or bye-law or in any collective agreement that I have been able to discover. There is, indeed, no evidence at all of its existence in any widespread form. It has been adopted occasionally for particular purposes—by the seamen once in the 1890's, and more recently by the restaurant-car staff in a local railway dispute, and it was spoken of, though not practised, in

connection with the Clyde Munitions dispute of February 1915. A variant of it appeared in the "four days a week policy" of the Scottish miners in 1914; but of this we shall have more to say hereafter. It is enough for the present to note that ca' canny, so far from being one of the recognised devices of Trade Unionism in this country, is very seldom employed and, when it is employed, is always met by fiery denunciations from the leaders of Labour.

(2) There are practically no Trade Union rules or bye-laws which regulate the amount of work to be done in a given time, though there are bye-laws, and, in a few cases, rules which regulate the distribution of a limited amount of work so as to afford work for all.[1] In the form of agreements for short time working for periods of slackness, such provisions for the distribution of work assume the character of collective agreements. These, however, have no connection with the charge of "restriction of output" arising from difference of opinion between employers and workmen as to what constitutes a fair day's work. If we judge by the employers' standard, there is, no doubt, a good deal of this type of restriction; but it rests, in nearly all cases, upon unwritten concert among the workers in a particular shop or locality, and there is very seldom, if ever, any sanction for it in the rule books or local bye-laws of the Trade Unions. Its purposes most often are either the general lightening of the daily task, or, under systems of payment by results, the prevention of cutting of piece-work prices or basis-time allowances.

(3) Restrictions on the manning of machines or the staffing of jobs may be imposed in any of the four ways described above. The rules of a Trade Union may forbid any member from helping to set, or conniving at the setting of, an unqualified man, or a man of another trade, on a job claimed by the Union for its members. Local bye-laws of the Unions may add to and elaborate these provisions, and members may be fined for breach of them. Collective agreements between Trade Unions and employers often specify the type of worker to be employed on particular types of work, and the methods of entry to the trade and promotion. There are, further, agreements between Trade Unions governing the demarcation of work between trade and trade, and in many cases, especially, in building and shipbuilding, the employers are also parties to these agreements. Lastly, restrictions on the manning of operations are often imposed by concerted action among the workers in a shop, district, or trade, without written agreements or regulations. In these cases the "restriction" is sometimes imposed by the official committee of a Trade Union in a district, and sometimes by spontaneous action among the men themselves. In the last case it is usually confined to a particular shop.

(4) The various regulations classified together under the fourth head may also be imposed by any of the four methods described.

[1] *E.g.* among the compositors.

Overtime is usually regulated by district bye-laws, and this applies also in many cases to restrictions on the working of payment by results, which, as we have seen, is also largely the subject-matter of Trade Union rules. Concerted action among the men in the workshop plays, in practice, an important part in this last type of "restriction."

How far are these "restrictions" justified? And, even if justified under existing conditions, how far are they, at best, necessary evils? If they are necessary evils, how far can the causes which make them necessary be removed? And, lastly, what effect does "payment by results" have upon them? These are the questions which we must next attempt to answer.

It is easiest to begin with an attempt at analysis of the motives which lead to the various practices described above. The workman in the workshop finds himself subject to a discipline, and to an ordering of the conditions of his work, which are outside his control. While he remains isolated, he is helpless in face of this discipline, and, however harsh it may be, he must either submit to it or leave his employment. Its actual incidence may be heavy or light, according to the type of employer, manager, and foreman with whom he has to deal; but, heavy or light, it is a discipline prescribed from without.

As soon as the individual workmen come together in an organised body, the position is to some extent changed. They are not, of course, any the less subject to the employer's discipline, but they are in a position to make common rules of their own, and so to modify the rules imposed by the employer. The employer still imposes the actual code under which they work; but, to a limited extent, they establish a veto upon his authority in certain matters.

Clearly, as long as the workers are unorganised and unresisting, the employer can impose upon them, if he so desires, very onerous conditions. He can, by fines and inducements, by rigorous supervision, or by the remorseless "sacking" of those who do not suit him, make the lives of his employees a burden. He can fix both rates of wages and piece-work prices or basis-times at his own sweet will, and can control with almost absolute precision the actual earnings of his employees from week to week.

To such conditions organisation furnishes the inevitable answer. The workers combine to secure, instead of earnings capriciously or at least arbitrarily determined by the employer, standard rates and established prices for their work. They combine also to resist speeding-up and overstrain, and to make the conditions in the factory more tolerable.

Here we have the most important set of reasons for the "restriction of output." Its primary object, we see, is to resist speeding-up in its two chief forms of price-cutting and overstrain.

(*a*) *Price-cutting*.—That the cutting of prices is a real grievance no one can doubt. Employers and social investigators agree with workmen in admitting that this is so. Indeed, in the past the practice has often been elaborately justified on several grounds.

Prices may be cut under a variety of circumstances:

(1) Where the job remains unaltered, but it is contended that owing to error the original price has been fixed too high.
(2) Where the job remains unaltered, but the worker produces more rapidly owing to familiarity with it, or to the presence of an inducement in the shape of a bonus or reward.
(3) Where the job is altered in such a way as, in the employer's opinion, to reduce the time necessary for doing it.

It will be seen that these different possibilities raise various points of social ethics.

(1) Where an error takes place in fixing the price for a job, it may seem that there is a clear case for readjustment as soon as the mistake is discovered. In practice, however, workmen find that the employer far more easily discovers when a price has been fixed too high than when it has been fixed too low. In nearly all shops the fixing of prices is unscientifically done, and the workman gets along by setting good jobs against bad. If the good prices are cut and the bad prices are not raised, it is clear that the workman's level of earnings is at once disturbed. The extent, therefore, to which prices fixed too high can legitimately be altered when the mistake is discovered depends, first, upon the degree of scientific accuracy with which prices are usually fixed in the shop, and, secondly, upon the readiness with which bad prices are raised to a fair level. The best way of dealing with the question is not to make mistakes at the outset.

(2) A quite different point arises in connection with the second set of circumstances. A workman whose output rises will naturally be inclined to claim that he should get the full benefit of his own increased efficiency, or at least that the benefit to the employer should be strictly limited to the saving on standing charges which increased production secures. The employer, on the other hand, will point to the burden of the competition with which he has to contend and to the benefit to the public in keeping prices down. The employer very often holds that a particular type of worker is "worth" so much a week, and that, subject to a certain payment for extra exertion involved in extra output, the worker ought to be satisfied with attaining this standard of earnings. If, then, the worker by producing more begins to exceed the standard and so to receive more than the market price for the class of labour concerned, the employer may argue that he has a perfectly good case for cutting prices. The remuneration of labour being determined by the law of supply and demand, he contends that there is no need to pay the worker more than he or she can command in the labour market.

It is now being widely recognised, by employers themselves,

that this argument is extraordinarily short-sighted, because it puts a premium on a restrictive policy. If the worker's price is to be cut as fast as he increases his output, he will be more than human if he does not keep down his output to the lowest limit that he can get the employer to accept.

This, of course, does not mean that obvious facts should be ignored. It does take longer to do a job the first time, or the first few times, than when the processes have become familiar, and there is, therefore, a good argument for a different price on new and accustomed jobs. This, however, should be secured by a special percentage allowance on new jobs and not by fixing a price and then cutting it as soon as the worker becomes proficient.

(3) By far the largest class of disputes about rate-cutting centres round cases in which it is contended that the materials, means, or methods of manufacture have been changed in such a way as to make the task lighter and capable of more rapid execution. It is sometimes provided in agreements dealing with the operation of systems of payment by results,[1] that there shall be no change in prices unless the methods of manufacture are changed.

Where this is the case, it is contended by Trade Unionists that the methods of manufacture are constantly changed for no other purpose than to make possible a cutting of rates, and that, when a real or fictitious change in methods takes place, the "cut" in the rate is often absurdly disproportionate to the actual lightening of the task.

The attempt is sometimes made to avoid the iniquitous abuse of the system by the further provision that, where the method of manufacture is changed, the alteration in price shall in no case be greater than the actual saving of time effected by the alteration in method. This is fairly easy to apply in cases in which the job can be divided into a number of distinct operations, to each of which a separate time can be assigned; but it is far more difficult in the case of jobs which cannot be so divided—*i.e.* on many of the jobs on which this form of rate-cutting most frequently occurs.

There is, moreover, a further moral question of importance arising in this connection. Ought the results of improved machinery or works organisation or better material or methods of doing a job to go to employer or to workman? Many of the same arguments occur in this connection as under the second heading. The employer who believes in the wage system, *i.e.* in the morality of purchasing labour power in the labour market at a price determined by supply and demand, will hold that any extra payment over and above the market rate is pure bounty, and that the workman has no claim at all to the product of his industry. Moreover, others who do not take quite this view will argue that in ninety-nine cases out of a hundred the improvement in methods or materials which lighten the job is not the result of Labour's work but of some person's

[1] *E.g.* Carlisle Memorandum of 1902 on the Premium Bonus System.

inventive capacity, and that not the workman but the employer who acquires the inventor or the invention has a good claim to any increased product that may result. To this the most effective answer would seem to be that it is a dangerous argument for the employer to urge. We may admit that often Labour does not cause the extra productivity, but neither does the employer, and therefore neither of them is entitled to the benefit, or disentitled to it, on that ground. The introduction of a labour-saving device into a particular occupation does not, on profound moral principles, entitle the workers concerned to the full benefit of the change, but it certainly does entitle them to share in that benefit, and their claim to a share is as good as that of the consuming public and far stronger than that of the employer.

We have now reviewed the various circumstances in which the cutting of prices most often takes place. We have next to ask how far the causes of restriction, in so far as they arise from the cutting of prices, are capable of being removed. We can only answer this question at present in the most general terms; for a full answer would involve the introduction of most of the matter contained in the later chapters of this book.

Price-cutting, under any capitalist system of production, is likely to be attractive to many employers. Labour cost being a part, and often a large part, of the cost of production, the employer is tempted to endeavour to save on it just as he endeavours to cheapen the cost of materials, plant, etc. There are two ways in which he can do this—by increasing output and so reducing the proportion of wages to standing charges, or by reducing piece-work prices. The second course has in the past usually seemed to the employer to be the simpler, and he has in many cases regularly practised it on every possible occasion.

Secondly, price-cutting is in some industries exceedingly easy. It is, in fact, easy wherever prices are not regulated by an elaborate and well-understood system of collective bargaining, such as in practice seldom occurs except on repetition work. Where prices are fixed for each separate job by individual bargains between the representative of the firm and the man or men who are to do the work, price-cutting becomes too fatally simple to be resisted. The workmen seldom keep accurate records of prices received, or compare notes fully enough to arrive at a common agreement concerning the prices to be accepted, and consequently firms are able constantly to manipulate prices to the disadvantage of their employees. Even when the attempt is made to fix prices in a more scientific fashion, by means of a special rate-fixing department, it is often the case that the science employed is the exclusive possession of the employer, and that most of the workers have no knowledge of the basis on which their prices are determined. In such cases rate-cutting may easily repeat itself in a more "scientific" form.

The suggestion usually put forward at the present time is that employers should promise not to cut rates without good cause, and that Trade Unionists should promise not to restrict output. If "restriction of output" in this suggestion refers only to deliberate ca' canny, there is a great deal to be said for it. No sanction will prevent ca' canny as long as the employer attempts to cut rates unfairly, but ca' canny would almost disappear if it became clear that employers and their representatives were prepared to play fair on the subject of earnings.

The phrase "restriction of output" is, however, as we saw, often given by the employers a very much wider interpretation. For instance, employers are inclined to argue that, if they promise not to cut prices unreasonably, the Trade Unions ought to be willing to abandon all restrictions on the adoption of payment by results—an argument which ignores the many Trade Union objections to payment by results which have no relation at all to the cutting of prices.

Moreover, even if the intentions of employers to turn over a new leaf in the matter of price-cutting are admitted to be sincere, it is not at all clear that they will be effective. Employers will not give, and can hardly be expected to give, an absolute guarantee that in no circumstances will prices ever be cut; nor have they yet succeeded in defining with any clearness the conditions under which prices may or may not be cut, or the extent to which they may be cut. I do not say that these difficulties are insoluble: I say only that they have not yet been solved, and that those "restrictions of output" which are maintained because of the fear of price-cutting are not likely to disappear merely as the result of an expression of good intentions on either side, or on both sides, but only as the result of the elaboration of far better methods of collective bargaining on all questions of prices and times under systems of payment by results.

(*b*) *Speeding-up*.—The grievances arising from "speeding-up" are often very difficult to dissociate from those arising from price-cutting, since price-cutting is one of the favourite forms of speeding-up. The two grievances are, however, fundamentally distinct; for workmen may object to speeding-up even if it is certain that their earnings will be very largely increased thereby. They may prefer the smaller earnings under comparatively easy conditions to high earnings made in an atmosphere of overdrive.

Speeding-up may take various forms, of which we can only indicate here a few of the most important:

(1) In cases in which the speed of the worker is largely determined by power-driven machinery, speeding-up may be effected by an increase in the speed of the machinery.

(2) Especially in time-work establishments, speeding-up may be accomplished by increased supervision, possibly accompanied by a system of payment by results for the supervisors only.

(3) Speeding-up is often accomplished by price-cutting.
(4) Other methods include the various devices of scientific management, *e.g.*, rest pauses, the elimination of "waste" motions, etc.
(5) Speed is sometimes maintained and increased by a policy of drastic dismissals of slow or inattentive workers.

The workers' reply to speeding-up is speeding-down. Just as there are many employers who speed up a willing worker and endeavour to get more than a "fair day's work," there are workers who endeavour to speed down a fair employer, and to do less than a fair day's work. The industrial system encourages this, and it is only surprising that it is not more frequent.

The working-class objections to speeding-up as such are very difficult to measure. In time-work trades the objection is constantly found that the employer is endeavouring to extract more work by means of extra supervision. It is less easy to say how strong the objection is among piece-workers; but it is at least clear that the resistance offered in many trades to the introduction and operation of payment by results is largely dependent on a preference for easy conditions of work to high earnings. This tendency becomes more marked when bonus systems or systems of scientific management are in question. Probably the working class has no common mind on the matter; but there is at least a very great volume of opinion which is opposed to speeding-up as such, and prefers a living wage under reasonable conditions to high earnings under conditions which preclude the enjoyment of them.

Just as we have seen that as long as the two classes of employers and employed remain there are likely to be two views of what constitutes a "fair day's work," so the controversy about speeding-up and speeding-down is insoluble under capitalist conditions. There is no automatic method of preventing employers from speeding-up or workers from speeding-down, and the extent to which either takes place will depend upon the economic relations of the parties. Far less than the narrower problem of fixing and readjusting piece-work prices is the problem of speeding-up capable of settlement by any kind of machinery. It is, in fact, a question, not of machinery, but of tact and temper.

To a great extent this is true of the whole problem of output. It need not be denied that output, especially on the more mechanical kinds of work, can be increased by the adoption of carefully devised systems of reward, but the incentive so secured may well be bought at too high a price if it proves to be completely destructive of good feeling in the workshop. Even if the type of work is suitable in itself for the adoption of a system of payment by results, smooth working is not likely to be secured for such a system unless piece-work prices or time allowances are fixed, under a well-regulated procedure, by collective bargaining.

If the truth of this statement is accepted, the consequence is clear. The way to secure the greatest and best output desirable is not that of flinging down the bulwarks erected by Trade Unionism, but that of giving to Trade Unions full recognition in the workshops as well as outside. Attempts to increase output by attacks on the British worker or by coercion of Trade Unionism will not succeed: better methods of dealing with questions of payment by collective agreement might well do away with many restrictive practices among both employers and workmen.

In speaking of "restriction of output" in this chapter, I have kept strictly to "restrictions" imposed, or said to be imposed, by workmen or their Trade Unions. I cannot, however, leave the subject without pointing out that "restriction of output" of the most conscious and deliberate kind is regularly practised by many groups of employers. There are many trades in which the hint of an impending fall in selling prices is enough to cause the employers, by open or tacit agreement, to limit the output of their works. Doubtless it will be urged that such restriction is only resorted to in order to prevent over-production; but it will surely be admitted that the employer usually finds his test of over-production in the selling price. If he thinks he can reap a larger profit by producing a large output at a low price, he produces a large output; if he thinks that a smaller output and higher prices will pay him better, he at once restricts output. Nor, unless such practices reach the dimensions of a Trust or Cartell, do they normally attract any attention—still less any reprehension. Indeed, even now employers are busy organising themselves, with Government encouragement, into associations which will certainly pursue this policy to an increasing extent. Yet any form of "restriction of output" by Labour is usually cried down, both by the public and by employers who themselves pursue these practices, as infamy of the worst sort. The plain fact, of course, is that, while capitalist production for profit and the wage system continue to exist, "restriction of output" by both employers and workers will also continue, though it may occur to a greater or less extent. But perhaps a moment's reflection will persuade those who are now so anxious to decry Labour for its restrictive policy that the argument really cuts both ways, and that workmen have at least as much justification for what they do as employer. In a sense, both are victims of a system, and, in a larger sense, the community is still more a victim.

CHAPTER IV

THE VARIOUS PIECE-WORK SYSTEMS

We have been content so far to use the term piece-work without attempting to define it; but before we begin to discuss it in greater detail, it is necessary that we should attempt to give greater precision to the terms which we shall have to employ.

"Piece-work" in the widest sense of the term implies simply that the employer is paying not so much per hour to the workers employed on the job, but so much for the job itself. A price is set on the job, and this price the employer pays. It is, then, for him a matter of comparative indifference to whom he pays it or how it is finally distributed. For the workmen, on the other hand, this is of primary importance, for the earnings of the individual workman depend not only on the price set on a job, but also on the distribution of that price where more workers than one are engaged upon the job.

One of the earliest uses of the term piece-work applied it to a system which we should not call by such a name to-day. The name of "piece-worker" used to be given to a sub-contractor who contracted with an employer to find the labour required for a job, received a lump sum from the employer in payment for that labour, and made his own terms with the individual workers whom he engaged. Thus, in the rules of the Amalgamated Society of Carpenters and Joiners (Rule 48, Clause 1), "sub-contractor" and "piece-worker" are treated as synonymous terms, and defined as meaning "a person taking the labour of a job only, and not supplying the material." In this sense of the term the "butty" or "contractor" in the mines, the piece-master in the engineering and foundry trades, the sub-contractor at the docks, and a host of others are piece-workers.

This, however, is no longer the regular usage of the word, and we are not concerned with systems that are neither more nor less than "sub-contracting." But it is important to emphasise the fact that there is a continuous series of varieties which leads from the "contractor" to the individual piece-worker in the ordinary sense of the word.

The "contractor," "sub-contractor," or "piece-master" has always been one of the worst enemies of Labour, and, as Trade Unionism has grown strong, he has been gradually eliminated. In most of the coalfields the "butty" system has disappeared; the worst forms of the contract system have been driven out from the iron and steel industry; the power of the sub-contractor at the docks is largely gone. In fact, the pure "contract" system, under which the engagement and dismissal of the vast majority of the workers employed, and the rate and amount of their remuneration, were in the hands of a few intermediaries between the firm and the workers employed in its works, has almost ceased to exist in any organised trade.

There are, however, still in force many systems which partake largely of its nature. Contract systems still exist in the coalfields of the Midland Counties, though the "butty" or "contractor" has now largely lost his control over the earnings of his subordinates. The spinner still engages and pays his piecers, big and little, and preserves considerable control over them, though the proportion of their wages to his is determined under a collective agreement. In the shipyards, in many engineering works, and elsewhere where working in squads or gangs is necessary, the charge-hand is still the intermediary between the management and the men, though in these cases wages and piece-work balances are most usually paid through the office in recognised proportions. At the docks the contract system is closely bound up with casual labour, and tends to disappear as casual labour is gradually reduced.

The transition from "contract work" to piece-work naturally follows the line of the various collective piece-work systems. There are many jobs which must be done collectively, and which, in their results, represent the co-operative labour of a number of workers. In many of these cases it is impossible to say how much work has been done by any individual workman, though it is quite easy to measure the product of the group as a whole. If, in such a case, it is desired to adopt a system of payment by results, there are only two ways in which this can be done. Either the whole group may be paid in accordance with the results of their co-operative work, or certain selected workers may be paid in accordance with the results of the work of the whole group, the rest being remunerated on a time basis.

The "butty" or "contractor" in the mines used himself to contract to get the coal out of a given seam, stall, or place at a tonnage rate, but used to pay the workers he employed at a day-work rate, reserving the difference for himself, and endeavouring to get a big output by driving his employees hard. This is the extreme case on the one side.

Collective piece-work in the Yorkshire dyeing industry offers one of the best instances of the other method. A "set" of workers includes men, women, and juveniles of very varying skill. Each of these workers has his or her time-rating. Any balance earned on piece-work is distributed through the office to the "set" in accordance with time-ratings and hours worked.

A middle case is that of the riveting squads in the shipyards. Here there are three classes of workers involved—riveters, holders-up, and helpers or labourers. The helpers or labourers are paid a time-rate, independent of the output or earnings of the squad; the riveters are paid a piece-price fixed by collective bargaining, in which the holders-up share in an agreed proportion of 10½d. to the riveters' 1s. Riveters and holders-up belong to the Boilermakers' Society; the helpers are enrolled in a general labour Union.

Collective piece-work, then, has many forms which provide a direct chain of connections between the most equitable and democratic systems at the one extreme, and the most iniquitous forms of "contract" at the other. The prevailing systems fall very largely into the middle class. In industries in which the craft spirit is not strong, or in which there is no wide gulf between skilled and unskilled, collective piece-work is most likely to assume a democratic form. In industries where Craft Unionism is strong, or the gulf between skilled and unskilled wide, the unskilled will often be ruled out from participation in any collective system.

It is worth noticing that the nature of a job may be such that it can only be paid for by results if a very large number of men share collectively in the proceeds. For instance, where there is night-work, a job may go on night and day with successive shifts, and the only practicable basis for payment by results may be for the day and night shifts to pool earnings. Or a job may call for the work of several separate squads of men in succession for different processes, and it may be thought desirable to pool as between these different squads. This, however, arises less often, and then mainly in connection with repair jobs, especially in the shipyards.

A further important variant of collective piece-work is altogether independent of the employer. This is "fellowship" piece-work, as it is often practised in engineering shops. In practically all engineering districts the recognised basis for collective piece-work is that all balances should be paid through the office in proportion to time-rates and hours worked. This may be done, but, when they have come outside the office, a group of men may prefer to "pool" earnings, and redistribute the balances on some mutually arranged basis, usually that of complete equality, irrespective of the hours worked. This "fellowship" system is usually confined to men of the same trade, and often to a small group of men who choose to work together upon it. It is, of course, purely voluntary, and "pools" and "fellowships" readily form and dissolve. A particular application of this system arises in shops in which some jobs are being done on piece-work and some on day-rates. In such cases the men in the shop sometimes arrange for certain men to do all the time-work jobs, but for all alike to share in the "pool" at the week's end.

It will be seen that the basis on which collective piece-work is applied may be either broad or narrow, and may range from two or three workers employed on a particular job to a whole department engaged on a complex series of quite different jobs. It is not possible to draw a sharp line of division at any point: but there is one distinction which is of importance. There is a clear difference in principle between what we may call "job piece-work" and what we may call "shop piece-work." In the former, the collective system is usually adopted because it is not possible to divide the product of a group of men employed on a single job—*i.e.* the narrowest practicable basis for payment by results is adopted. In the latter, the reason for a collective system usually lies not in the impossibility of individual payment by results, but in the desire to provide a collective stimulus to output for the whole shop, in preference to a series of distinct stimuli to individual workers in the shop.

The Trade Unions have, for the most part, no clearly defined attitude on the question of collective piece-work. Where the work in question is "squad" work, which must of its nature be done collectively, the Trade Unions usually prefer some form of collective payment, though this preference is not necessarily for a democratic system. The Craft Union may prefer a basis of payment which leaves the unskilled worker on day-rates. Rule-books and local bye-laws of engineering Trade Unions frequently insist that "wherever practicable, piece-work shall be worked collectively, the balance to be apportioned in the office to each individual concerned on time worked and wages paid."[1] This type of regulation, however, is not usually interpreted as entitling the unskilled worker to a share in the balance.

On the question of shop piece-work, Trade Union opinion is far more difficult to ascertain. Some Trade Unionists express the view that it is merely an employer's device to save on the cost of supervision by getting the workers to speed one another up; but such a criticism is hardly of value unless it also takes into account the respective desirabilities of being speeded up by supervisors appointed by the employer or by the public opinion of the workshop. Some employers, again, express the view that shop piece-work would completely fail to afford any stimulus to production and that the public opinion of the shop would be more likely to favour speeding-down.

As against this view, on the Trade Union side the statement comes in this case from Messrs. Gallacher and Paton, two Clyde engineers, and both active in the forward movement. The contention of the authors is that the way to advancement for the

1 A.S.E. London District Bye-Laws. See also National Society of Coppersmiths, Rule Book, Rule 33.

workers lies through the strengthening of Workshop Committees consisting of Trade Unionist representatives. They then proceed to sketch out a policy for the proposed Committees when they have been established. First, they suggest the concentration in their hands of all negotiations about piece-work prices or basis-time allowances. They then proceed to discuss the problem with which we are at the moment concerned. The relevant passage deserves quotation in full:

"Only the apathy or disloyalty of the workers themselves can prevent the Works Committees having in a very short time the experience and the authority to enable them to undertake in one large contract, or in two or three large contracts at most, the entire business of production throughout the establishment. Granted an alliance with the organised office-workers—a development which is assured so soon as the Shop Committees are worthy of confidence and influential enough to give adequate protection—these contracts might include the work of design and the purchase of raw material, as well as the operations of manufacture and construction. But, to begin with, the undertaking will cover only the manual operations. The contract price, or wages—for it is still wages—will be remitted by the firm to the Works Committee in a lump sum, and distributed to the workers by their own representatives or their officials, and by whatever system or scale of remuneration they may choose to adopt. A specially enlightened Trade Union would no doubt elect to pool the earnings of its members and pay to each a regular salary, weekly, monthly, or quarterly, exacting, of course, from the recipient a fixed minimum record of work for the period."[1]

Thus we find that, from very different points of view, a system of shop piece-work finds favour both with some employers and with the revolutionary Trade Unionists of the Clyde. It is true that the employer usually proposes to go on paying wages to each individual worker through the office, whereas the Paisley memorandum suggests a collective payment to the Works Committee; but, important as this difference is, the suggestions are, in their most essential feature, the same.

Common as the various systems of collective piece-work are, nothing like the same number of persons is found working under them as works under systems of individual piece-work, *i.e.* systems under which each worker is paid according to his or her individual output over a given period or for a given job.

To these systems of individual piece-work we must now turn. As we have seen, the conditions of individual piece-work differ very widely indeed from case to case. Individual piece-work prevails among some of the most highly skilled and highly paid

[1] Quoted from *Towards Industrial Democracy: A Memorandum on Workshop Control*, by W. Gallacher (Clyde Workers' Committee) and J. Paton (A.S.E.). Published by Paisley Trades and Labour Council, 1917.

classes of workers, and on the other hand it is found also amongst some of the most sweated and underpaid workers, especially among women. It will be necessary at the outset to speak separately of these two classes, although it must be borne in mind that they are not clear and distinct, and that there is an infinite gradation of types and classes of workers between them.

As we saw in an earlier chapter, the conditions of piece-work differ to some extent according to the nature of the product and the process concerned. Where the product is easily measurable in terms of some natural unit of output—tons, yards, etc.—and where the methods of production are so highly standardised that a given amount of energy and dexterity from a given worker can be practically relied upon to produce a given output, the piece-work price tends entirely to overshadow in importance, if not altogether to eliminate, the question of the time-rate. In these cases, if the piece-work prices are adequate, the worker is practically assured, under all conditions, of securing an amount of money commensurate with the time taken, the skill used, and the energy involved. This, as we have seen, is the position in some of the processes in the iron and steel industry, in most processes in the cotton industry, and in a number of other cases.

On the other hand, where the process and the product are not standardised, and where there is no such universal unit of measurement, the mere fact that piece-work prices are on a reasonable basis is not enough to ensure that the worker will receive, week in and week out, a fair level of remuneration. In these cases, therefore, the time-rate will remain important, even when the piece-prices have been fixed on an agreed basis. In the engineering industry, for instance, at any rate among the skilled workers, piece-work and payment by results generally are only admitted on condition that a guarantee is given that the time-rate of the workers concerned will be paid in all cases irrespective of output. This principle of a guaranteed time-rate, which is generally recognised in the engineering and kindred industries, is obviously capable of more general extension, and ought, as we shall see, particularly to be extended to many of the underpaid trades which work on payment by results.

Given his time-rate, the engineering worker can proceed to bargain about the level of piece-work prices. This he can usually do by insisting that piece-work prices shall be fixed on such a basis as to yield on the average, or as a minimum, a certain percentage over and above the time-rate. Thus, in negotiations for the extension of piece-work, or for the revision of piece-work prices, it will often be found that the first step is to get the employers concerned to agree that piece-work prices ought to be fixed on such a basis as to yield at least 33⅓ per cent on day-work rates, or some other percentage ranging from 20 per cent to 50 per cent. In fact, where the Trade Unions are well organised, they habitually refuse to agree to any piece-work prices which cannot be shown to conform to these conditions.

It will be noted that where this is done, as it is throughout the engineering industry, the worker is only guaranteed his day rate, but the prices are fixed at such a level that he ought to be able to earn at least a given percentage above that rate. There is no guarantee that he will, or that any individual will, actually earn such a percentage. It has sometimes been suggested that such a guarantee ought to be insisted upon, and it has been stated by Mr. and Mrs. Sidney Webb that such a system was actually put into practice over twenty years ago in several factories, when piece-work was first introduced. The suggestion is that a guarantee should be given that every worker who is working piece-work shall be paid at the end of the week at least time and a quarter, or time and a third, irrespective of his actual output, or of the average output of the whole group. It will readily be seen that this would, in effect, create a distinct and higher time-rate; and it is stated by Mr. and Mrs. Webb that piece-work normally demands greater intensity and effort from the worker, and that therefore the worker who works piece-work ought to be actually guaranteed a higher rate of earnings than the time-worker whose normal intensity of work is less. This argument does not seem conclusive. Surely the right way of dealing with the problem is to guarantee the day-work rate, and then to fix piece-work prices at so high a level that the extra intensity of work is fully rewarded. The system suggested of a guarantee to the piece-worker of a higher rate, irrespective of output, is open to two objections, one from the employer and one from the time-worker.

The employer would urge with truth that if he guaranteed the time and a third, this would merely mean that piece-work intensity would only begin when the worker had passed the level of production necessary to earn time and a third, and that many workers would prefer to continue working at day-work intensity, drawing their time and a third at the end of the week, and not putting any special intensity into their work for the sake of earning what would probably be only a small further balance above their guaranteed rate.

This brings us to the objection from the time-worker's point of view. This objection is twofold: if what we have suggested above took place, there would be created two classes of workers working at time-work intensity—the nominal time-worker, who would be guaranteed only the day-rate, and the nominal piece-worker, who would be guaranteed the higher rate. This would be obviously unfair to the time-worker. Moreover, it is not fair to assume that the only difference between time-work and piece-work is one of intensity of effort. Time-work is preferred in many cases because the job that is being done is not capable of accurate measurement, or because quality is of more importance than quantity in output. The time-worker may, in many cases, be of the most skilled type, and may be doing the most important work of all, and it is obviously unfair where this is the case that he should receive what is virtually a lower day-work rate than the piece-worker, who may be engaged on less important work. Indeed, it has even been suggested that where men are kept on time-work they ought to be guaranteed a higher day-work rate, in order to bring their earnings more into conformity with those of piece-workers, and that was the principle on which the 12½ per cent bonus, granted to time-workers by the Ministry of Munitions in the autumn of 1917, was based. This second course is no less open to objection from the Trade Union point of view, as a general practice, than the first course. Any differentiation in day-work rate between the time-workers and the piece-workers is necessarily liable to break up the solidarity of the Trade Union which includes them both, and on this, as well as on the other grounds stated above, it seems most necessary that a uniform guaranteed day-rate for time-workers and piece-workers alike should be preserved. If a higher level of earnings all round is desired, the remedy is to increase this guaranteed day-work rate and not to give to any special class of workers the guarantee of a special percentage upon it.[1]

So far we have been dealing merely with certain general problems which affect individual piece-workers as a whole. We must now come to some of the more special problems which affect the piece-workers in particular trades. In this chapter we shall confine ourselves to a broad description of a few of the general systems involved. Subsequent chapters will enlarge upon many of the points involved, and will deal with them from a critical, as well as a descriptive point of view.

Broadly speaking, individual piece-workers in strongly organised trades may be divided into two general classes, those who work under an agreed written price list, and those whose piece-prices are fixed from time to time by "mutuality" or special bargain. In many trades there exist written lists of prices setting out in elaborate detail the rates to be paid for certain operations, either for turning out a single article or, in the case of smaller operations, dozens or hundreds. These lists naturally vary very much in complexity from one to another. The most complex of all—the cotton weavers' list—is a document which only the initiated are able to understand, while some of the simpler trades are able to work satisfactorily on a quite short and easily understood list of a few pages. Naturally the piece-work list occurs principally, if not entirely, in relation to operations which are of a standardised

[1] This of course does not apply in cases in which the particular worker or group of workers are offered a specially high rate on the grounds that they are engaged upon work calling for special responsibility or skill. This practice is common in the engineering industry, and seems to the present writer eminently desirable as long, at any rate, as any system of payment by results or differentiation in earnings between one worker and another continues to exist.

character, or which can at least be reduced to standard elements. Where the work varies widely from job to job, or from day to day, it is almost impossible to compile a regular written list, although it may be quite possible to put in writing the general principles on which prices are to be fixed for individual operations. Piece-work lists exist throughout the mining industry, in iron and steel, in most of the textile industries, the boot and shoe industry, sheet metal trades, and certain other smaller branches of metal work; in certain types of transport work, especially the coal trade, and the handling of pit-props and timber, and other standard types of cargo, and in many other cases. Where they exist, they represent naturally an enormous economy of labour on the side both of the employer and of the workmen, since they eliminate more or less completely the day to day bargaining about piece-work prices which exists in the organised trades where no written price lists have been agreed upon.

The most notable example of an industry in which piece-work exists on a large scale without written lists is in engineering, where the principle on which piece-work prices are fixed is known as that of "mutuality." This means that, in the words of the National Engineering Agreement of 1907, "the prices to be paid are fixed by mutual arrangement between the employer and workman or workmen who perform the work." This principle of "mutuality" in effect operates in very different ways in different cases. Usually the employer is represented, so far as the fixing of piece-work prices is concerned, by the foreman, or, in shops in which specialisation has to be carried further, by a special Time Study expert or Rate-Fixing Department. On the other hand, in some shops the individual workman does carry through the bargain on his own account, although there is necessarily always a certain amount of informal consultation between one workman and another on the subject of piece-work prices, and a certain amount of accumulated knowledge among the workmen as to the levels at which prices have been fixed on previous occasions for the same or similar jobs.

In other shops there is a more definite system of collective bargaining on piece-work prices. Sometimes the workmen keep a complete record of all prices which are fixed, and thereby establish a regular basis for collective bargaining. Sometimes Shop Committees exist which directly bargain about any piece-work price which is in dispute with the representatives of the management. This last was especially the case during the war as the shop-stewards' movement grew in strength and directed its attention to the problem of piece-work prices.

With these safeguards "mutuality," thus elastically interpreted, may work well in the case of highly organised workers engaged upon jobs which are not of a repetitive character, and for which, therefore, the fixing of price lists is difficult if not impossible. "Mutuality," however, operates very differently when it is applied to less skilled workers who have less cohesion one with another, and far less bargaining power in the face of the employer. This brings us to the problem of piece-work in the less organised trades.

The establishment of an agreed list of piece-work prices represents a considerable Trade Union achievement, and it is therefore not surprising that such lists are seldom found in the less organised trades. In these trades the great majority of piece-workers work under systems prescribed by their employers, often without even the smallest pretence of Collective Bargaining. The employer arbitrarily lays down the rates to be paid, and the worker has no alternative but to accept these rates or leave his employment. Of course, the situation is better in some cases than in others, and there is, in fact, a continuous series from the most highly organised piece-work trades to the worst examples of sweating and subcontracting; but it is easy to see that where there is no strong Trade Union in the background to enforce the claims of labour, a piece-work system lends itself to abuse more easily even than a day-work system. Thus, it is very seldom, if ever, that piece-workers in an unorganised trade have their day-work rates guaranteed. Such a guarantee is the result of an insistence by the Trade Union that a minimum standard of life shall be assured to every worker. The employer who is not confronted by a Trade Union is not likely to impose such conditions upon himself. Moreover, unorganised workers have no safeguard against rate-cutting; not only can the employer fix the rate at whatever level he chooses, but he can also vary it arbitrarily or even capriciously if he so desires. If he goes to very great lengths he may, of course, provoke a revolt even among unorganised workers, and there is always the chance that such a revolt may lead the workers to organise. But short of this extreme he is master in his own establishment, and can, if he so desires, juggle with piece-work prices to almost any extent.

The worst extremes of unregulated piece-work are naturally found in the case of women workers. There are few cases outside the cotton industry in which men and women have received equal piece-rates; even in the woollen industry, for instance, the women receive lower piece-work prices than the men in many districts for identical work. In the majority of cases, however, women are not employed on identical processes with the men, and where this is so their position tends to be even worse than in cases where men and women work side by side, since they lose even that protection which is afforded by the men's collective endeavours to protect themselves. In the purely women's trades piece-work is usually regulated only in the most rudimentary fashion; and even in industries in which the men have secured comparatively elaborate piece-work lists, such as the boot and shoe industry, women's prices remain very largely unregulated.

The war has in many respects led to a considerable improvement

[1] Note, however, the effect of the Trade Boards Acts, see p. 91.

in the position of piece-workers in those trades in which, before the war, comparatively little regulation of piece-work conditions had been secured. This is particularly the case in the munitions trades, in which the war has very greatly improved the position both of semi-skilled and unskilled male workers and of women. Side by side with these prices and improvements has gone organisation in Trade Unions; but even despite the extraordinary growth of Trade Unionism among the less skilled men and the women during the last few years, their position with regard to Collective Bargaining is still lamentably weak, and little has been done to establish the regulation of piece-work conditions on a collective basis. Even the promises of equal piece-work rates made so lavishly by the Government and incorporated in the Circulars and Orders regulating wages under dilution, did not, in practice, secure equal pay, especially in the case of the women workers. If the conditions were so unsatisfactory during the war, when the strategic position of Labour, so far as wages were concerned, was relatively favourable, it is clear that enormous difficulties will appear as soon as these artificial conditions are removed.

Piece-work, then, in the unorganised trades is usually exceedingly unsatisfactory from the point of view of Collective Bargaining. It is not, however, implied in this statement that the majority of semi-skilled or unskilled workers tend to favour time-work as against piece-work; in fact, the reverse is very often the case, and piece-work often finds favour among the less skilled trades. The reasons for this are obvious. The unskilled worker or the worker in an unorganised trade is usually in receipt of only a very low rate of earnings, which is not in any sense a reasonable living wage. He or she is therefore compelled to accept anything which offers even a small increase in earnings, and, if even quite unfair and unreasonable piece-work conditions offer these small inducements, they are likely to find a ready acceptance in preference to time-work, which, indeed, where the workers are unorganised, may be made just as onerous as piece-work by excessive supervision and speeding up. A second reason why less skilled workers in many cases favour piece-work is because they find themselves working in competition with skilled craftsmen who are earning piece-work balances, while they themselves are excluded from any share in those balances. Such a system whereby skilled and less skilled workers co-operate on a particular job, but the skilled workers work piece-work, and the unskilled on day-rates, is obviously quite unfair, since the piece-work intensity at which the job is presumably done is inevitably extended to the less skilled, as well as to the skilled workers; in fact, such a system means for the less skilled workers piece-work intensity at a time-work rate.

CHAPTER V

BONUS SYSTEMS IN GENERAL

We have now surveyed in general outline the various piece-work systems which are principally in vogue in this country, leaving for subsequent consideration certain fancy systems which fall rather under the head of "Scientific Management" or "Efficiency Engineering." We have now to deal with the other main method of payment by results—the system under which the worker receives some form of bonus dependent upon output. These systems are infinitely various in character, and it would be quite impossible to attempt any exhaustive enumeration of them, since almost every manufacturer who adopts them at all likes to work out his own system to suit his special fancy. All that we shall be able to do, therefore, is to describe the general characteristics of such systems and the general elements of which they are made up.

Bonus systems are not of course necessarily or universally dependent upon output. For instance, in many works, the principle of a time-keeping bonus is adopted, *i.e.* the worker is paid a bonus provided he or she has worked a certain number of hours during the week or over a longer period. Time-keeping bonuses, as such, do not concern us in dealing with payment by results, but it is necessary to mention them because in some cases a bonus which is calculated on output is in addition made dependent on time-keeping. Thus, however big an output the worker may produce during the week, there are some factories in which he is not entitled to any bonus unless he has put in a certain number of hours of work, and there are others in which the bonus is reduced in proportion to the number of hours avoidably lost. This, however, is only an excrescence on the system of paying bonus on output, and need not detain us further.

Bonus systems, like piece-work systems, may be either individual or collective. The individual worker may be paid a bonus on his or her individual output over a period of time or on a particular job; or a group of workers may be paid a collective bonus on their total output. In the second case the principles and proportions on which the bonus is allocated to the individuals included in the group may vary widely from case to case, as under systems of collective piece-work.

The commonest type of individual bonus system is one under which the bonus begins when a specified output has been reached. Under this system the worker is paid a time-rate, and to this time-rate there corresponds a certain nominal task, which, however, is not enforced as a minimum. Until this task has been accomplished no bonus is paid; but on all output over and above the given task a certain bonus per piece is added to the worker's earnings. Or, in other cases, a lump sum is paid as a bonus to all workers who reach the standard output. This is an instance of an individual bonus system superimposed upon time-work conditions. Another system is one in which the bonus is superimposed upon piece-work. The worker is paid a piece-work price on his or her output, but again when the output reaches a certain level per hour or per week, a bonus is added either on the whole of the earnings, or on all additional production over and above the stipulated standard output. As we shall see in a later chapter, this system, in one of its forms, coincides with Taylor's differentiated piece-rate system.[1]

These are the main types of individual bonus payment; but of course there may be almost infinite variation in the actual systems adopted. There may be not only special additional bonuses on time-keeping, diligence, good conduct, etc., etc., but also special deductions not merely for spoilt work, but for other classes of misdemeanour. It will often be found that, where an individual bonus system is applied to strongly organised workmen, the method established is that of offering an extra reward for good and efficient work, rather than that of imposing a penalty for bad or inefficient work; whereas, in the case of sweated or unorganised trades, the employer may, by arbitrary deductions, reduce the actual earnings of the worker considerably below the level of earnings nominally secured by the piece-work prices.

Individual bonus systems, although common, present no special features, and are not of special importance, except in the cases dealt with in the next two chapters. We reserve these cases—the Premium Bonus System and the various "efficiency" systems—for special treatment.

Collective bonus systems, on the other hand, present many features of interest, and are coming more and more into favour with employers at the present time. In case after case such systems were adopted in the industries producing munitions during the war, largely in factories producing in bulk a highly standardised type of product under conditions which admit of accurate measurement of effort in terms of output. As in the case of collective piece-work, collective bonus systems can cover a wider or narrower group of persons. The systems which are most coming into vogue at the present time are what are usually known as shop bonus

[1] See Chapter VII. page 59.

systems, or works bonus systems. That is to say, they are systems under which the bonus is paid on the total output of a shop or department, or even of a whole works. The usual method of establishing such a bonus system is something like this: first, an attempt is made to ascertain the normal output of the shop or works for a given period of time, say a week; this normal output is ascertained by taking the figures for a certain period during which the shop has been engaged on the work in question, either under time-work or under piece-work conditions. The ascertained average, or some total based upon it, is then taken as the standard output for the works. The bonus may then be paid, either on all output in excess of the standard, or on all output in excess of a given percentage of the standard output, the addition being either on a flat rate for all such excess, or on a graduated scale rising as the total output increases.

Such a collective bonus based on shop or works output is usually adopted in substitution for all other systems of payment by results. This, however, is not necessarily or universally the case, since the bonus may be paid on top of other piece-work or bonus earnings calculated on an individual basis. Where, apart from the collective bonus, the workers within the group are time-workers, the bonus is extended to certain classes of men who are not themselves directly producing the output on which the bonus is paid, *e.g.* supervisors, inspectors, setters-up, maintenance men, etc., etc. Where some of the workers under the collective scheme are also individual piece or bonus workers, the collective scheme is often extended to cover not only these workers, but also the time-workers employed in the shop, the bonus being paid to all alike, usually in proportion to their time-rates. Sometimes the collective bonus system even assumes what appears at first sight to be the somewhat fantastic form of paying one group of workers a bonus on the output of another group. This, for instance, is the case with certain tool-room bonuses in the engineering industry, where, over and above their time-ratings, the workers in the tool-room are paid a collective bonus on the output of the shop on the ground that their work is necessary to that of the machine-minders, who are directly producing the output, and that this output in the last resort depends on the speed and efficiency of the work done in the tool-room.

We now come to the difficult task of describing the differences and resemblances between piece-work and bonus systems. One difference is on the surface obvious. The piece-work system is a system in which the worker or group of workers is paid so much per piece, so that the total earnings vary exactly with the total output produced. Twice the output means twice the wages, and so on.[1] Bonus systems, on the other hand, are methods of applying an incentive to extra output without necessarily making the total

[1] This is, of course, often modified by the concession of a guaranteed time-rate.

earnings vary exactly in proportion to the output produced. Thus, under a bonus system, if an output of twenty produces a wage of 20s., an output of forty may only produce a wage of 25s., or may, on the other hand, produce a wage of 50s., according to the system adopted. This difference, however, while it is important, may in some cases be illusory. The present writer has known and worked through highly elaborate bonus systems which cannot be understood without considerable labour, but which, when they are reduced to their elements, are found to be merely piece-work systems expressed in a more roundabout way. What the managements which establish such systems believe to be gained by this form of obscurantism it is impossible to guess; but the ways of the price-fixing experts of many firms are past all understanding.

There is one other complication which ought to be mentioned in relation to some of these bonus systems. In a few cases the bonus is calculated, not simply on the output of the shop, but on the selling price of that output, or even on the profits realised by the firm through its sale. In these cases bonus systems pass over into profit-sharing systems, which are dealt with in a later chapter.

This is not the place to attempt any general summary of the conditions under which bonus systems are worked, since, for a general estimate of their value, we require to take into account not simply the variations which we have so far described, but also the more scientific or pseudo-scientific systems which will be described in the next two chapters. When we have dealt with these we shall be in a better position to offer some general observations upon bonus systems as a whole.

CHAPTER VI

THE PREMIUM BONUS SYSTEM

THE Engineering Agreement of 1901 contained the following clause relating to piece-work:

PIECE-WORK [1]

Employers and their Workmen have the right to work piece-work.

The prices to be paid for piece-work shall be fixed by mutual arrangement between the Employer and the Workman or Workmen who perform the work, and the Employers guarantee that they shall be such as will allow a Workman of average efficiency to earn at least his time-rate of wages, with increased earnings for increased production due to additional exertion on his part.

The Federation will discountenance any arrangement or re-arrangement of prices which will not allow a Workman to obtain increased earnings in respect of increased production due to such additional exertion, and the Trade Unions will discountenance any restriction of output.

The Federation agree to recommend that all wages and balances should be paid through the office.

A mutual arrangement as to piece-work rates between Employer and Workmen in no way interferes with the Trade Unions arranging with their own members the rates and conditions under which they shall work.

In the following year the question of the Premium Bonus System, which was not included in the above terms, came suddenly to the front. Trade Unions in a number of districts had already for some time been offering strenuous resistance to this new system, which was explicitly based on the desire to reduce labour costs while maintaining earnings by means of increased output. As the result of a purely local reference on the question, the matter was brought up at Central Conference between the Amalgamated Society of Engineers and the Engineering Employers' Federation, and in August 1902 a provisional agreement was made and signed by these two bodies. Under this agreement the Engineers accepted the Premium Bonus System on a national basis, subject to the safeguards incorporated in the agreement.

The text of the agreement, usually known as the York Memorandum, contains the following recommendations made by the

[1] In 1907 this clause was replaced by a new one, which considerably improved the position by giving an absolute guarantee of day-work rates. See Appendix A.

Employers' Federation to their constituent firms (but not, it should be noted, in any way binding upon them under the terms of the agreement):

1. The time-rate of wages (for each job) should in all cases be paid.
2. Overtime and nightshift to be paid on the same conditions as already prevail in each workshop.
3. A time limit, after it has been established, should only be changed if the method or means of manufacture are changed.
4. No firm should establish the bonus system without intending to adhere to it.

Subject to these very inadequate safeguards, the Premium Bonus System was thus accepted by the principal Society in the engineering industry. Naturally, the acceptance did not pass without question, and many adverse comments were passed by members of the Society, while the action of the A.S.E. was strongly resented by other Societies, which found their resistance to the system prejudiced. Mr. G. N. Barnes, then general secretary of the A.S.E., was strongly in favour of the system, and he called in to his assistance a powerful ally in the person of Mr. Sidney Webb, whom we find writing in the A.S.E. journal of October 1902 strongly in support of the adoption of the system. Mr. Webb stated that he " believed the system to be a good one for Trade Unionism." He dwelt on the " evils of competitive piece-work in the engineering trade," and said hard things of what he called the " crude and primitive device of payment by the hour," a system which he also described as " a most unscientific and inaccurate method of remuneration." Mr. Webb expressed his preference for a piece-work list system, but, realising that this was a system for which neither employers nor workmen were prepared, he expressed the view that the Premium Bonus System was, in the circumstances, " an admirable expedient." He therefore congratulated the Executive on its achievement, and strongly urged the members to ratify the provisional agreement.[1]

Naturally, this endorsement was at once seized upon by the advocates of the system. The *Engineer* had for some time been running a campaign in its support, and had secured a letter from Mr. G. N. Barnes lending his adhesion. The articles in the *Engineer* were principally directed to explaining to employers that the Premium Bonus System offered an opportunity of reducing labour costs, though they also included arguments directed to showing to workmen that earnings would be increased as well as output. The *Engineer* at once incorporated the letters of Messrs. Barnes and Webb, together with its own articles, in a pamphlet which had a wide circulation.

[1] This, of course, would not represent Mr. Webb's view to-day. His advocacy of the Premium Bonus System was based upon the extraordinarily unfavourable nature of the piece-work systems which then prevailed.

Nevertheless, Trade Union opposition by no means died down, but rather continued to gather force as the system came more widely into operation and as attempts were made to extend it to a wider range of trades. In 1909 a resolution strongly hostile to the system was carried at the Trades Union Congress, and the Parliamentary Committee of the Congress was instructed to call a conference of the Societies concerned with a view to the abolition of the system. This Conference in turn appointed a Committee of investigation, which took evidence from many trades and districts, and finally made a report of an exceedingly hostile character.

It proved, however, impossible to secure united action for the abolition of the Premium Bonus System, although the majority of trades and districts continue to resist its application in their own case. It went on spreading slowly right down to 1914, and during the war its extension has been accelerated to a slight extent. There are a few districts, including Barrow-in-Furness, in which it is not generally disliked; but, for the most part, Trade Union opposition to it remains, with good reason, as implacable as ever. It is now time to explain the working of the system itself.

The Premium Bonus System, thus inauspiciously introduced into this country under a collective agreement in 1902, is an attempt to adopt payment by results and at the same time to avoid some of the most obvious disadvantages of the piece-work system from the employer's point of view. It was, in the early days of the system, always a strong point of the employer that it was strictly *ex gratia*, and that if a man did not like to receive a bonus he could go on working on time-rates. This meant that a few men began by accepting the bonus, and that most of the rest almost inevitably followed suit, when they saw that higher earnings were being made. At the same time the employer, by maintaining his attitude that the system was *ex gratia*, was able to resist any demand for collective bargaining on the subject of basis times and allowances.

We must now proceed to a direct account of the system itself. The general principle is this: instead of fixing a piece-work price for the job, the employer fixes a "basis time" in which the job ought to be accomplished. If it is accomplished in less than the "basis time" the workman is paid, over and above his standard time-work rate, a bonus proportionate in one way or another to the time saved. The effect of this method of payment is that, under all the systems except one, the labour cost of the job to the employer falls with every increase of output, while at the same time the earnings of the workman increase, but not in proportion to the increased output.

The simplest system is that originally introduced by Mr. F. A. Halsey, an American engineer, and usually known as the "Halsey System." Under this system the workman is paid a fraction, usually either one-third or one-half, of the time saved, or, what comes to the same thing, is paid a bonus at a fixed rate for every hour saved. Thus, supposing the time allowed for an operation is 12 hours, and a workman, whose time-rate is 1s. an hour, does it in 8 hours, he will be paid at his time-rate for either 2 or 1⅓ hours, according to the system adopted ; or alternatively he will be paid for all the hours saved at either one-half or one-third of his time-rate, *i.e.* 6d. or 4d. Whichever the nominal method adopted the result to the workman will be exactly the same.

This system has only the merit of simplicity. The second system, which has been probably more widely adopted in this country, and which has certainly been acclaimed by employers as a great new discovery in engineering, is known as the "Rowan System." The principle of this system can be expressed in two ways : the simplest is to say that for every 10 per cent that is saved on the time allowed the workman receives a 10 per cent increase in earnings : the more complicated way is given in the formula which is usually adopted by those who desire to explain the system.

$$\text{Bonus} = \frac{\text{time saved}}{\text{time allowed}} \times \text{time taken.}$$

It will be seen that, under all these systems alike, the actual labour cost of the article to the employer decreases as the workman increases his output ; but in order to make this quite clear a Table is appended, showing how the two systems work out in practice in terms of a job for which ten hours are allowed.

			Halsey (50 per cent basis).		Rowan.	
Time allowed.	Hours taken.	Hours saved.	Hourly Earnings.	Labour Cost of Job.	Hourly Earnings.	Labour Cost of Job.
10 hrs.	10	0	10d.	100d.	10d.	100d.
	8	2	11.25d.	90d.	1s.	96d.
	5	5	1s. 3d.	75d.	1s. 3d.	75d.
	3	7	1s. 9.66d.	65d.	1s. 5d.	51d.
	1	9	4s. 7d.	55d.	1s. 7d.	19d.

This calculation of the labour cost of the job, *i.e.* what are the equivalent earnings per piece on piece-work, assumes that the basis time under the premium system is a real and not a fictitious time. In fact, however, the basis time is usually lengthened to allow of a premium being earned. That is to say, it is a fictitious standard, and the comparison is made in order to show that it is such.

The fourth column in this Table gives the hourly earnings under the Halsey System (50 per cent basis), and the fifth column the labour cost of the job to the employer under this system ; while the next two columns give the corresponding figures for the Rowan System. It will be seen that the Rowan System is the more favourable to the workman until half of the time allowed for the job has been saved, but that as soon as this point has been passed the Halsey System becomes immensely more favourable. Thus, under the Rowan System the worker's earnings are automatically limited to something less than double time; for, since every 10 per cent of the time saved gives only a 10 per cent increase in wages, it is clear that, in order to make 100 per cent on day-work rates, the workman will have to save 100 per cent of the time, that is, will have to do the job in no time at all. Under the Halsey System, on the other hand, while the bonus rises more slowly at the start, there is no upper limit, and, if the effect of the adoption of the system is a great increase in output, the workman's earnings may soar far above double time. This, however, is of course not the usual case, although it takes place in isolated establishments and on isolated jobs. The argument put forward in favour of the Rowan Bonus System as against the Halsey System is this: Premium Bonus Systems are often being instituted in shops which have previously worked either under time-work conditions or under conditions of the most unscientific piece-work. Where this is the case there is a large margin for possible errors in fixing the standard times in which the jobs are to be done. The effect of this, under the Halsey System, is that on certain jobs workmen earn very high wages indeed—as wages go in these days: thereupon the employer, it is urged, is under an absolute necessity of cutting the rate if he is to meet the competition of other firms. But as soon as he does this his workmen become resentful, and may in many cases resort to a policy of deliberate restriction of output—or so the employer says. Employers usually urge that the Rowan System is to be preferred because it is not open to these objections. This was, in fact, the burden of a very useful book on the Premium Bonus System which was first published by the *Engineer* about the time that the controversy was raging round the system in 1902 and 1903, and has since been several times reissued and amended.

Under the Rowan System, it is often said, the price cuts itself: the workman's earnings being naturally limited to something less than double time, however much out the employer may be in his calculation of the standard time required, nothing very dreadful can happen; for the workman cannot go out with "extravagant" earnings at the end of the week. Therefore it is urged that while, up to the right point, the Rowan System provides the maximum incentive, and is actually more favourable to the workman than the Halsey System, it has the great advantage from the employer's point of view that it is absolutely impossible under this system for the employer to overpay his workmen or to have any inducement to cut the rate.

It is now time to look at the Premium Bonus System rather more from the point of view of the workman. It will be seen that, in all the cases hitherto discussed, the greater the workman's output, the less the labour cost per article to the employer. Under a straight piece-work system, as we saw in the previous chapter, the labour cost of an article does not vary whether the output is large or small, provided only that the minimum quantity required to cover the guaranteed time-rate is manufactured. Under the Premium Bonus System, on the other hand, as under most bonus systems, the more work the employer can get out of the workman, the less he has to pay for that work; for by paying for only a proportion of the time saved—one-half or one-third, or some other fraction—he pockets for himself, or passes on to the consumer in the form of a reduction in price, the remaining portion of the saving. Nor is this the only advantage to the employer. It is well known that a high output per man and per machine per hour is profitable to the employer, because by means of it he saves considerably on his overhead charges, and utilises the plant in his factory in the most economical way possible. Thus, if the employer is paying the workman half the time saved, he is not only reducing the labour cost of the article manufactured by the other half of the time saved, but also the "oncost" by the reduction in other works charges which almost invariably accompanies an increase of output.

This fact naturally causes resentment among the employees, and leads them to object strongly to what they call the "dishonesty" of the Premium Bonus System. The employer points out, in return, that he is, after all, bound by the competitive conditions in his industry: rival manufacturers are doing their best all the time to cut down their labour costs in order to undersell him by placing the article on the market at a lower price, and thus giving the consumer the benefit, or at any rate a share of it. The employer therefore contends that the other half of the time saved and the reduction in overhead charges do not remain in his hands, but are passed on to the consumer in the form of a reduction in price. No doubt there is, in some cases, truth in this argument, but a general willingness by the Trade Unions to regard it as conclusive would, it seems, prevent them from seeking any improvement in their present position under the wage system.

Some employers take a different line in replying to criticisms of the Premium Bonus System. They point out that, while it is correct in theory to say that the workman is only paid for a part of the time saved, this can readily be remedied by making an exceedingly generous time allowance for the job, and so enabling the workman to earn more. Thus, supposing a job takes a workman 10 hours to do at "payment by results" intensity of work, then, if the job is timed at 12 hours, and a bonus is paid at the rate of half of the time saved, the workman will only get an hour's extra payment, whereas if 14 hours are allowed the reward is at once doubled if the rate remains the same. Thus the mere system adopted is no key to the earnings that may be made, since it is necessary to know, not simply at what rate the bonus is being paid, but also how generously the time allowances are being fixed. Everything depends in the last rèsort upon the time allowance which is arranged. This is proved very conclusively by the actual experience of the Premium Bonus System in certain centres, notably

Barrow-in-Furness. At Barrow the workman has usually been able to earn a good percentage on his day-work rate, because the time allowances give a good margin. This being so, he has not bothered his head, as a rule, about the fundamental justice or injustice of the system under which he is working: he has looked at his money at the end of the week, found it fairly satisfactory, and accepted the system which brings him such results.

This, however, does not alter the fundamental fact that the Premium Bonus System, whether it be the Halsey variety or the Rowan variety, does rest upon an unjust basis. It may be possible to correct the injustice by falsifying the times allowed, but a system which creates an injustice in order to remedy it by a falsification can hardly be regarded as satisfying the conditions required of a reasonable method of wage payment.

There is, indeed, one variety of the Premium Bonus System which is not open to the objection stated above. This is the variety in which the workmen is paid for the whole of the time saved. In these instances the bonus system becomes exactly equivalent to piece-work with a guaranteed day-rate. It is simply another way of calculating piece-work prices by expressing them in terms of times taken and saved, instead of directly in terms of quantities manufactured.

The fact that, where the workman is paid at his day-rate for the whole of the time saved, the Premium Bonus System coincides with piece-work, shows more clearly than anything else what is its fundamental object. Both the Halsey and the Rowan Systems have primarily in view a reduction in the labour cost of the article manufactured; they seek to secure an additional output from the worker, and at the same time to pay him less per piece for that output.

It has been implied in much that we have said already during this chapter that the Premium Bonus System raises many problems from the Trade Union point of view. We have seen that the employers began by claiming that the introduction of the system was strictly *ex gratia* on their part, *i.e.* that the granting of the bonus was a purely voluntary act of the employer, and that the workman was not entitled to it as a part of his wages. It was a "little present" which they made to him at the end of the week if they liked his work, and as such it formed no part of the wage contract, and was not recoverable at law as a part of wages. It followed that on the subject of standard time allowances and the fixing of Premium Bonus conditions there could be no collective bargaining, since collective bargaining would imply the recognition of the system as a part of the contract, and not a mere act of grace on the part of the employer. Naturally this extraordinary attitude could not be long retained in its entirety. The employer was, in effect, claiming that, provided he paid standard day-work rates, any further remuneration which he might choose to give was entirely a matter for himself, with which the workmen and their Trade

Unions would have no concern. The great dispute concerning the adoption or rejection of the Premium Bonus System in 1902 centred largely round this point, and the agreement signed by the Amalgamated Society of Engineers, in which they accepted the system under certain safeguards, provided for a very limited amount of collective bargaining. It did recognise the system as more or less on the same footing with piece-work, and in the intervening years there has been a closer and closer approximation of the two systems so far as collective bargaining is concerned.

This does not mean that collective bargaining in dealing with Premium Bonus basis times has been fully established, since, as we shall see in a later chapter, collective bargaining is by no means fully established in the industries in which the Premium Bonus System has been introduced, even as regards ordinary piece-work. It does, however, imply that if satisfactory conditions for collective bargaining about payment by results can be introduced at all into these industries, they are likely to apply to the Premium Bonus System and the other " Efficiency " systems which we are about to discuss quite as much as to ordinary piece-work.

CHAPTER VII

EFFICIENCY SYSTEMS OF PAYMENT

We have been dealing so far with systems of payment by results without reference to the methods employed in arriving at piece-work prices or basis times. We come now to those systems which rest upon some "scientific" method of ascertaining the length of time which a job ought to take, and the methods by which the job ought to be done. In the following chapter we shall survey briefly certain of the wider implications of Scientific Management: here we desire to deal with Scientific Management only in so far as it has resulted in the evolution of new systems of payment by results.

The Scientific Managers claim that all the systems which we have described in earlier chapters, including piece-work and bonus systems, individual or collective, and the Premium Bonus System in its various forms, are fundamentally "unscientific" in that none of them rests upon a "scientific" method of fixing prices. They very reasonably urge that the result of such slipshod systems is that there is a wide margin of error in all cases, and that the prices fixed for jobs are in some cases inadequate, and in other cases far too liberal. The result, they maintain, is that the workmen are always trying to force prices up, while the employer, if his workmen make large earnings as a result of liberal piece-work prices or basis times, is continually attempting to cut the rate, and thus bring prices down to a level more in keeping with what he regards as the workmen's proper standard of living.

"Rate-cutting," the advocates of Scientific Management proclaim, can be prevented and made entirely unnecessary by the application of scientific method. They hold that if, instead of fixing the piece-work price by guess-work or merely basing it upon previous experience of operations under time-work conditions, the firm bases its prices upon a detailed study of the operations and the methods of performing them, there is no longer any but the smallest room for difference of opinion concerning the correct rate for the job, and therefore no reasonable pretext either for the workmen to endeavour to get the prices raised, or for the employer to cut the rate.

Under ordinary piece-work or bonus systems the Scientific Managers claim that something like the following conditions are continually recurring. A piece-work price or basis time is fixed for a job. The workmen thereupon do the job in considerably less than the time allowed. Upon this the employer cuts the rate so as to bring the men's earnings to what he regards as a reasonable percentage over their day-work rate. Thereupon the men retaliate by means of "ca' canny." The next time the job is done they take even longer perhaps than the time originally allowed. The employer is then compelled once more to increase the time allowed, and, when the circle has been completed, the process begins all over again. This is no doubt an exaggerated description of what happens in an ordinary piece-work or bonus shop; but this, or something like it, does undoubtedly happen in a considerable number of cases.

As we have stated, the remedy of the advocates of Scientific Management is to fix prices or times only after a detailed study of the job. This study they aim at making mainly by means of two methods: time-study and motion-study. Before a job is priced an expert rate-fixer will overlook the doing of the job under ideal conditions by a selected worker. He will note the time taken not merely for the operation as a whole, but for all the various parts of which the operation is made up—the handling time, the machine time, and not merely these in general, but handling and machine times divided into the greatest possible number of distinct but connected operations. The worker selected should be, the Scientific Managers urge, a good average man, not a specially fast or skilled workman, but one well above the ordinary run of the shop. A study of this kind will be repeated a number of times with the same or different workmen and on the same or different machines. When a sufficient mass of data has been accumulated, the experts will proceed to work out the time that ought to be allowed for the doing of the job. They will add together the various times taken for the particular parts of the operation under test conditions, and will make an allowance of so much per cent on the total time taken, or perhaps different percentages for machine time and handling time. These allowances will be made in order that the time fixed for the job may not be the least time in which the job can be done by a good workman under ideal conditions, but may allow a margin sufficient to enable the ordinary worker engaged from day to day upon the job to make upon it a percentage over and above his day-rate.

This method of time-study is often strongly resented by workmen. The method usually is for the foreman, probably with an expert from the Time-Fixing Department of the works, to stand over the man who is doing the job with a stop-watch, timing each operation or part of an operation. The men hold that in many cases the worker who is to do the job is unfairly selected, in that a man very much above the average is chosen by the management, and claim further that the data accumulated in this way are freely used by the management for the purpose of speeding-up. The management learn by the method of time-study what is the shortest time in which a job can conceivably be done, and they then endeavour to bring the whole of their workers up to the efficiency which they regard as proper for the job, irrespective of the fact that the capacity of one man for rapid work is very much greater than that of another. Scientific Management experts, of course, strongly exhort employers not to adopt such tactics, that is to say, not to use the results of time-study for speeding-up; but under present-day factory conditions, in which the principle of collective bargaining over piece-work prices has hardly been established, there is obviously a very strong temptation for the employer to act in this manner. There is a still stronger temptation, naturally, for the foreman or departmental manager who wishes to make a success of his job by showing a low labour cost for the article produced, and who does not realise the economy of high wages.

The other method adopted by Scientific Management experts is that of motion-study. They aim, not merely at seeing how quickly the worker can do the job if left to himself, but also at regulating the way in which the job is done, in order to secure that it shall be done in the minimum possible time and with the minimum number of motions. For this purpose they employ what is known as "motion-study," the object of which is so to study the motions of a workman engaged upon a particular job as to know what motions are of a wasteful character, and can be eliminated with advantage. Where this method is adopted, once again the job is studied by experts who stand over the workman while he is doing it. The motions employed are carefully observed, and thereafter suggestions are made with regard to the motions that ought to be used in doing the job, the tools with which the job can be done with least effort, the adjustments proper for these tools, etc. When the job is issued with the price upon it, instructions covering these points are issued with it, and the price placed upon it is such that it is only by following instructions and eliminating waste motions that an adequate percentage over the day-work rate can be earned.

For and against this system a great deal has been said. It is possible, Scientific Managers have pointed out, that a hundred workers in a shop engaged upon a relatively simple operation will have a hundred different ways of doing it, whereas one of these ways is undoubtedly the right way in the sense that the job can be done as well, and in less time, by one method than by any other. It is urged that, if the workers are told which is the right method, they will all reap an advantage by following this method, in that they will be able to turn out more work, and thereby to increase their earnings. On the other hand, it is urged against the system that it tends to convert the workman into a mere automaton, to take away from him even that freedom of choice which the machine system of production has left to him in the past, and to reduce what have been skilled jobs to the level of mere unskilled machine operations. The skilled workman in the factory, as in the recognised arts and crafts, values his own methods of doing his job, and is not prepared to take without question the command of an expert.

Sometimes the Scientific Managers attempt to meet this point by issuing the results of time-study not as definite instructions, but merely as advice, and by leaving at least skilled workmen to follow or not to follow the suggestions as they think fit. This, however, can hardly prevent prices from being fixed on the basis of the job being done in the way suggested, and in this case it does not meet the objection that the worker may easily, under this system, be reduced to an automaton. Such automatism may result not merely in depriving the workman of all pride in his labour, but also in placing an undue strain upon him, both mentally and physically, thereby using him up more quickly, and finally flinging him upon the industrial scrap-heap. A story which illustrates this point very well was told by Miss Isabel Sloan on her return from a journey to America in the course of which she visited many of the famous Scientific Management factories. In one factory the manager pointed out to her a workman who seemed to be working with great efficiency and at top speed. "That," said he, "is our best worker. Of course he is just a little feeble-minded."

By the aid of time- and motion-study the Scientific Management advocates claim that they are able to fix prices and times with such justice that no question of rate-cutting need afterwards arise. In particular, they claim that their method of time-study enables them to avoid one of the most frequent difficulties with regard to the cutting of rates. Piece-work and bonus agreements have in many cases included a clause that in no case shall the rates to be paid for the job be changed unless the materials, means, or methods of production are altered.[1] This clause, which is intended as a safeguard against rate-cutting, has in fact proved in the past singularly ineffective, since there is no guarantee that when a slight change in the method of production or the materials used occurs, the rate will not receive a drastic cut, out of all proportion to the actual change effected. Indeed workmen often declare that changes of method are introduced for no other purpose than that of cutting the rate. In order to meet this objection, the Scientific Management firm is sometimes prepared to give a guarantee that all cuts in the rate resulting from changes in method shall be exactly proportionate to the change involved. This they are able to do, they claim, because their method of time-study has already divided the job into the smallest possible component parts, so that they know, not simply the normal time for the job as a whole, but the time required for each particular part of the job. They are thus

[1] *E.g.* Carlisle Premium Bonus Memorandum.

able to guarantee that when a change affecting any part or parts of a job occurs, the cut in rate shall affect only the times allowed for those particular parts of the job which are affected by the change. In this way it is impossible, they claim, to make a disproportionate cut, as has been so often done under piece-work conditions, or under the Premium Bonus System.

That this argument possesses considerable force no one is likely to deny; but it is necessary to point out that its force is entirely conditional upon the workers in the shop being in full possession of the data on which prices are based, and being in a position to apply the method of collective bargaining to the fullest extent.

The workers have shown themselves almost uniformly opposed to the methods of time-study and motion-study which have been described above. Here and there an individual workman has been found who has no objection to the system, or even who likes it; but collectively the workers have demonstrated a permanent opposition which has been particularly marked on the part of the more skilled type of workman. In the unskilled groups organisation is weak, and the sense of pride in work very much less developed, so that employers have found it comparatively easy to apply conditions of motion-study and time-study, where they have thought fit to do so. This applies particularly in the case of women workers engaged on purely repetitive processes. In the case of skilled workmen, although there has been a considerable application of the system in the United States, it has so far only touched a very small number of workers in this country. It has increased considerably during the war period; but even now it has been mainly applied to the less skilled types of work, and more particularly to repetition work.

It is now time to look rather more closely at a few of the main systems put forward by leading advocates of Scientific Management. Taylor, the founder of Scientific Management, had a system of his own which claims pride of place both because of its historical priority and because it is perhaps the most iniquitous system existing. Taylor called his system "the differential piece-rate system." His method was to fix two distinct piece-rates for the same job, and at the same time to fix a standard output per hour. When the worker reached or exceeded the standard output, he or she was to be paid on the higher piece-rate. When the worker fell below the standard of output, he or she was to be paid at the lower piece-rate. Day-work rates were not to be guaranteed. Thus, the inefficient worker not merely earned less in proportion to his or her lower output, but was actually penalised in addition for being inefficient, so that it was barely possible for a worker of less than the standard efficiency to earn a living wage. This indeed was Taylor's object, and he claimed for his system the sovereign merit that it would weed out the inefficient. He urged that the principles of Scientific Management should include, not merely the fixing of the proper time to be taken for a job, but also the selection of the proper worker to do that job, and this he proposed to secure by means of the survival of the fittest. By rewarding the efficient and penalising the inefficient, he hoped to secure that the process of " unnatural selection " would leave only the efficient workers in the factory, and force the inefficient to seek work elsewhere, possibly on jobs more suited to their particular capacities. The case for his system is thus quite clear; but its operation under the wage system and in a Capitalist environment leaves much to be desired. The inefficient worker, instead of being weeded out, may continue in the factory at a miserably low rate of wages, or may merely, when he or she is weeded out, be flung on the unemployed market. This indeed has happened in the case of many firms which have professed to follow Taylor's principles, although no doubt Taylor would have been the first to repudiate their discipleship.

The second system to which attention must be directed is that put forward by Mr. Gantt, specifically in order to correct the possibilities of injustice in the operation of the Taylor System. His system is " the task and bonus system." Ostensibly, it differs from Taylor's System in that it recognises only a single piece-rate, and includes a guaranteed minimum rate of earnings. Like the Taylor System it begins by fixing a standard task, say five " pieces " an hour, and it then fixes a price per piece, say 2d.: and the hourly rate is then 2d. × 5 = 10d. This hourly rate is guaranteed, irrespective of output, but the worker who reaches or exceeds the standard task receives a bonus, say of 30 per cent, on the piece-work price. The effect of this system is that there is a sharp leap in earnings, as under the Taylor System, when the standard task is reached, and also a guaranteed minimum below which the worker's earnings cannot fall. At the same time, although there is nominally only a single piece-work price for the job, there are, in effect two prices, or rather, the nominal piece-work price is not the actual piece-work price in the case of any worker who reaches the standard output. The 30 per cent bonus which is added to the earnings of any worker reaching the standard in effect creates a differential piece-work price, of exactly the same character as that which is openly advocated by Taylor. A comparison between the Taylor and the Gantt Systems in terms of the labour cost of the job will serve more clearly than anything else to bring out their essential points of resemblance and difference. It will be seen that, if the earnings of the workman under the two systems are expressed in terms of the labour cost of the job to the employer, *i.e.* of the equivalent piece-work price for the job, the only difference between the two systems so expressed lies in the guaranteed day-rate under the Gantt System.

[TABLE

Number of Pieces made per Hour.	Taylor System.		Gantt System.	
	Earnings per Hour.	Labour Cost to Employer.	Earnings per Hour.*	Labour Cost to Employer.*
1	2d.	2d.	10d.	10d.
2	4d.	2d.	10d.	5d.
3	6d.	2d.	10d.	3.3d.
4	8d.	2d.	10d.	2.5d.
5	1s. 1d.	2.6d.	1s. 1d.	2.6d.
6	1s. 3.6d.	2.6d.	1s. 3.6d.	2.6d.
7	1s. 6.2d.	2.6d.	1s. 6.2d.	2.6d.

* *I.e.* a bonus of 30 per cent on a time-rate of 10d. per hour is paid on the worker attaining to the standard output of five pieces per hour

This Table shows clearly certain things which the Gantt System is so devised as to conceal. In the first place, although the price per piece is nominally uniform, there are in effect two (or in certain refinements of the system, more than two) piece-work prices, and the price is only uniform for those workers who reach or exceed the standard task. In the second place, Gantt's guarantee of the day-work rate is to some extent illusory, in that what is guaranteed is not in fact the real day-work rate at all, but a rate lower than that of the worker who reaches, but does not exceed, the standard output. In fact, the system only differs from straight piece-work with a guaranteed day-rate in one respect—that it does not guarantee a real day-rate, but only a fictitious rate lower than the real rate. In this respect it reaches by a crooked road a result similar to that which has been reached by certain Arbitration Tribunals under the Munitions Acts during the war, by guaranteeing to the piece-worker only a fictitious day-rate lower than that of the time-worker.

The method of payment associated with the name of Harrington Emerson is far more complicated than that of either Gantt or Taylor. The Emerson System also sets a standard task and guarantees a time-rate irrespective of output. Its distinctive character lies in the detailed graduation of the *efficiency bonus* by which it rewards greater output. Under this system every range of output is graded as a degree of efficiency. The standard output as determined by time-study is treated at 100 per cent efficiency, and every lesser output is graded as a smaller percentage of efficiency. A time-rate (say 10d.) is fixed, and this is guaranteed in all cases. At a fixed percentage of the standard efficiency (say 61 per cent) a bonus is granted, and this bonus increases in geometrical progression as the worker approaches the standard efficiency, after which it proceeds by arithmetical progression. A table will serve to make this clear. Suppose the hourly rate guaranteed to be 10d., and the standard task five "pieces" per hour, the Table will then read :

Percentage of Standard Efficiency.	Bonus per cent.	Earnings per Hour.	Labour Cost per Piece to Employer.
60	0	10d.	3.3d.
67	½	10.05d.	3d.
73	1	10.1d.	2.8d.
76	2	10.2d.	2.6d.
79	3	10.3d.	2.6d.
82	4	10.4d.	2.5d.
85	5	10.5d.	2.47d.
90	10	11d.	2.44d.
95	15	11.5d.	2.42d.
100	20	1s.	2.40d.
101	21	1s. 0.1d.	2.39d.
105	25	1s. 0.5d.	2.38d.
110	30	1s. 1d.	2.36d.

It is clearly shown by this Table that, under the Emerson System, the labour cost of the job, *i.e.* the equivalent piece-work price, slowly falls as the output increases. A time-rate is guaranteed ; but, as in the Gantt System, this is a fictitious time-rate considerably below the rate paid for the standard output.

The three systems so far described are all of American origin, and have not been widely adopted in this country in their pure form. There are, however, many systems based upon them and closely resembling them which are in operation in various works in this country. For instance, certain works, both in America and in Great Britain, have attempted a further elaboration of the Taylor and Gantt Systems by providing, not as they did, simply for two piece-work prices, but for a further differential piece-rate when a still higher level of output is reached. Thus, under such a system there is set, not merely a standard task with the accomplishment of which a special bonus is paid, but also a higher task which carries with it a further bonus when the higher level of output is attained.

On the whole, however, British manufacturers have tended rather to take the Emerson efficiency task as a basis and to base upon it various modified efficiency systems which aim at securing similar results. The essence of the Emerson System is that the bonus paid for efficiency begins at a comparatively low point, and the stimulus is thus afforded to even the less efficient types of workers. This feature is reproduced in many of the British systems, especially in those which are designed for repetitive jobs, and above all in those which are designed for women. In a recent book advocating a system of this type under the name of " the reward system," Mr. Henry Atkinson gives a number of charts illustrating different varieties of the system.[1]

These systems are practically all modifications of the Emerson System, in that they are based upon a reward beginning at a certain

[1] Henry Atkinson, *A Rational Wages System*, G. Bell & Sons, 1917, 1s. 6d.

percentage of efficiency, usually 62.5 per cent, but sometimes 75 per cent, or 80 per cent: they also reproduce the Taylor and Gantt characteristic of a sharp leap in earnings when 100 per cent of efficiency is reached, and they provide, at least nominally, like the Gantt System, for a guaranteed day-rate. Three of these systems are here set out for purposes of illustration:

System I. Day-rate guaranteed. Reward begins at 62.5 per cent efficiency. Half the time saved paid for from 62.5 per cent to 100 per cent efficiency. Two-thirds of the time saved paid for at over 100 per cent efficiency (*i.e.* there is a sharp leap in earnings at 100 per cent efficiency). Reward reaches 30 per cent on day-work rate at 100 per cent efficiency.

System II. Day-rate guaranteed. Reward begins at 62.5 per cent efficiency. Half the time saved paid for throughout; but a lump sum bonus of 5 per cent given to those who reach 100 per cent efficiency. (Under this system the rise in earnings is less sharp at 100 per cent efficiency, and there is only a single rate of allowance throughout.) Reward reaches 30 per cent on day-work rate at 100 per cent efficiency.

System III. Day-rate guaranteed. Reward begins at 80 per cent efficiency. All time saved paid for throughout; but a lump sum bonus of 10 per cent given to those who reach 100 per cent efficiency. Reward reaches 25 per cent on day-work rate at 100 per cent efficiency.

It should be noted that Mr. Atkinson does not regard all the varieties of the reward system as equally suitable to all operations. He regards it as desirable to find a system specially suited to each general class of operations. Thus, different systems will be required for jobs which are mainly of a machine character, or jobs in which the machine very largely sets the pace, and in jobs of a handling character, or jobs in which there is a large margin for variations in speed, according to the methods pursued by the particular worker who is doing the job. Further different variations will be required in some cases for highly skilled workmen, and for unskilled workers on pure repetition work.

It is now time to say something more generally with regard to all these efficiency systems as a whole. We have seen the objections which are raised by the workers to the methods of time-study and motion-study, and it can hardly be denied that under present conditions these objections have at least a considerable validity. It may seem all very well that the employer should ascertain exactly the time which is required for the doing of every job, but the situation is complicated by the fact that the employer generally claims to ascertain this time without reference to the workers' opinion, and to insist that his own opinion, or that of his expert, with regard to the time that is necessary, shall prevail. Clearly no such one-sided determination of reasonable times can be regarded as equitable.

If the methods of time-study are to be even considered at all by the workers there must be the fullest form of collective bargaining with regard to the determination of all times allowed.

Even collective bargaining, however, would probably not suffice to reconcile the workers to time-study, and still less would it be likely to reconcile them to the methods of motion-study.

Motion-study naturally takes different forms, and assumes varying degrees of importance, according to the nature of the operation in question. It has reached the largest proportions in purely manual operations, such as the classic instance of loading pig-iron on to a truck, or the laying of bricks, or sewing by hand in a tailoring establishment. In such cases an attempt is made to standardise the operation, so that it is performed in the least possible number of motions, or in the shortest possible time, or with the minimum of effort. These, obviously, may not all mean the same thing. The speeding-up of an operation by the elimination of useless motions may involve either more or less effort, or the number of motions may be increased while the time is diminished. The accusation has been made that in many such cases the employer gets a greater output by placing a far greater strain on the worker, who may even be worn out by overdriving and thrown on the scrap-heap like an old machine. The object of motion-study is indeed largely that of making the worker into a machine.

In the case of machine operations, the effect of motion-study may be rather different. In such a case, the machine itself, in proportion to its automatic character, dictates the actual motions to be used in working it, and motion-study is therefore most likely to suggest an alteration or adaptation of the machine, sometimes such an alteration as to remove work from a skilled to a semi-skilled or unskilled category. Apart from this, however, some Scientific Managers carefully prescribe even for skilled craftsmen the motions and methods to be employed on complex machines and operations. Here, again, then, the tendency of Scientific Management is towards standardisation of both machines and men.

The workmen's objection, then, to motion-study would be quite intelligible, even apart from the fact that the present system of control of industry makes workshop bargains inevitably to some extent one-sided and arbitrary. To the results of time- and motion-study, and to the systems of payment by results which are based upon them, there are many further objections. In the first place, in their actual working the systems are never anything like as "scientific" as they profess to be. The investigator who goes into any Scientific Management shop with a fair understanding of his business will soon find that in practice the hard-and-fast principles laid down by the Scientific Management experts and "efficiency engineers" require very considerable elasticity in working. He will find that times cannot, except on the simplest operations, be set with perfect accuracy, that all sorts of unforeseen difficulties occur in the shop and impair the accurate working of the system, that jobs have to be done sometimes on machines which are perfectly suited to them, and sometimes on machines which are less perfectly suited, that interruptions inevitably occur in the course of doing a job, that one worker inevitably delays another, or that the workshop organisation to some extent breaks down, and that finally even the most scientific time-fixing experts make big mistakes. He will therefore soon see that, when the scheme comes to be worked in practice, it is generally necessary to adopt on a fairly large scale a system of allowances, in order to get over these difficulties. For one or another of the above reasons the worker does not, on the efficiency or reward system, earn the balances which have been expected. Where the management desires to deal fairly by the workers it tries to put the matter right by making special allowances on the time given, or merely by paying the workers extra sums by way of "allowances" on the completion of the job. Even a casual survey of time cards in a shop working on the efficiency system will serve to show how large a part these allowances almost necessarily play in adjusting the theoretical principles of efficiency engineering to actual workshop conditions.

Clearly such allowances open the way to considerable abuses. Even if collective bargaining with regard to piece-work prices and standard times is fully established it does not follow that collective principles will apply in dealing with the question of allowances. These, therefore, continue to depend largely upon the goodwill of the management, or, if goodwill is absent, upon constant friction in the workshop. This applies less, as we have seen, in the case of simple operations which it is comparatively easy to time accurately, than in the case of more complicated operations; but it is a fact largely fatal to the more extreme projects of Scientific Managers who desire in the name of science to make "reward systems" generally applicable to all classes of operations.

A further strong objection to "efficiency" systems from the workers' point of view is that they often result in highly complicated methods of payment, which are unintelligible to the ordinary workman. Only the simplest forms of the systems advocated have been described above: and these in themselves would be enough to baffle many workers. But in practice every disciple of the masters of the movement has his own system, so that methods vary from shop to shop, from department to department, and from job to job. The result is that, in the majority of cases, the workers do not try to understand the system under which they are being paid, but simply judge it by the amount of money they receive at the end of the week. The objection to this state of affairs will be obvious to any one who has even the smallest belief in the value of self-government. It concentrates knowledge in the hands of the expert, and leaves the governed with only the vaguest conception of the system that controls them. This is in itself enough to condemn all methods of payment too complicated to be easily understood by the ordinary worker.

Scientific Management experts often claim that their systems are not really complicated, and that there is no reason why the workmen should not readily understand them. There is some truth in the first of these contentions, for the systems are in many cases capable of being expressed in comparatively simple terms. Any one, however, who has seen the methods usually employed in efficiency shops for the calculation of bonuses and rewards, and the time-cards which are given to the workers as an explanation of their earnings, will soon realise that the majority of Scientific Management experts either do not go out of their way to make the systems intelligible, or at any rate do not succeed in making them so. Indeed, it would seem as if some of them go very far out of their way in order to describe their systems in the most roundabout and unintelligible way possible.

It has often been suggested by Trade Unions in connection with systems of payment by results that the workmen should be allowed to retain copies of the instruction cards which are issued to them in connection with the various jobs done on payment by results. To this many employers offer the strongest opposition, advancing as a reason that if they allow the workman to retain a copy of his instruction card this will inevitably get into the possession of other employers, who will thus learn the labour costs of their rivals. This tendency to secrecy in the workshop is, I believe, misguided, even from the employer's point of view; but in any case it should not deter the workers from claiming the right to retain copies of their cards if they think fit. In some cases, especially where Shop Committees exist, the method adopted has been that of allowing the Shop Committee to retain and file copies of all instruction cards that are issued, in order that they may be used as a basis for collective bargaining on future jobs. This indeed does furnish a way round the difficulty in many cases, and we shall return to it in the chapter in which we deal with the function of Workshop Committees in connection with payment by results.

Unintelligibility, or even difficulty of comprehension, is by itself a sufficient objection to any system of payment; even if it is possible for the workers, by taking infinite pains, to understand the system on which they are paid, it is highly undesirable that they should be put to this trouble. Indeed, it is absolutely certain that, where a system difficult to understand is in operation, the great majority of the workers will not take the trouble to understand it, but will judge of its effects simply by the total amount of their earnings at the end of the week. This, again, will result in making it very difficult to establish any principle of collective bargaining in the fixing or adjusting of prices, and will thus once more bring the workers back to purely individual systems of bargaining, and deprive them of the control which they ought to have over their workshop conditions.

Another point which cannot be too strongly stressed is that the claims put forward by a few Scientific Management experts, and in particular by Mr. Taylor himself, that their systems do away with the need for collective bargaining, have not the smallest foundation. Mr. Taylor contends that, when once Scientific Methods of fixing times and prices have been adopted, payment by results is no longer a matter for collective bargaining, but merely a matter for cold science, and that there can be no difference between employer and workman with regard to the proper prices and times for each job. At the same time Mr. Taylor assumes without any argument that the expert who fixes prices will be the servant of the firm, paid by the firm, and doing the firm's work. How he can expect a man who is employed by the management and paid by the management to be so completely impartial that there is no need for collective bargaining, or to be accepted by the workers as so completely impartial, he barely deigns to explain. Clearly, although Scientific Management methods may reduce the possible margin of error in determining piece-work prices, they cannot altogether remove it, and even if the time that ought to be taken for a job is clearly established a further complication at once confronts us. All the time-study in the world cannot show how much ought to be paid for a job. It can only show at most the length of time a job ought to take. That is to say, it cannot determine what is to be the standard of living or of remuneration of the workers. Piece-work prices are inevitably fixed in relation to an assumed standard of living of the worker employed, and time-study gets one no further towards the determination of this standard. Whether the hourly rate should be 10d. or 10s. or £10 no amount of time-study can decide. An hourly rate, or at least a standard of living must be fixed or assumed before the Scientific Manager can set his system of payment to work, and, as there can be no Scientific Method employed in fixing such a rate, the rate is essentially a matter for bargaining on a collective basis. This, indeed, is only another way of saying that Scientific Management has only devised a further method of payment under the wage system.

Some Scientific Managers may object to this statement on the ground that, by a combination of time- and motion-study, they can determine the varying degrees of skill, attention, etc., required for various jobs, and thereby arrive at a justly graduated scale of wage-rates. This adjustment, however, is purely relative, and assumes a standard rate or rates as already in existence. We may say that A's skill is twice as great as B's, and we may conclude that we ought to pay A twice as much as B ; but this will not help us to determine how much we ought to pay either of them. Nor is it really possible, in the last resort, to measure degrees of skill by any such quantitative standard.

Most advocates of Scientific Management would now admit a good deal of what has been said in this chapter ; but it is important to make the last point clear because it destroys, once and for all, Taylor's claim that Scientific Management does away with the need for bargaining about wages, and substitutes law for force in the determination of wage-rates. It does, and can do, nothing of the sort ; for it does not, and cannot, touch the question of the proper division of the product between Labour and Capital, or of the propriety or impropriety of any such division. Scientific Management does nothing to remove the need for collective bargaining and Trade Union organisation.

CHAPTER VIII

SCIENTIFIC MANAGEMENT

In the last chapter we dealt with certain methods of payment which are closely connected with the system of Scientific Management. In this chapter it is necessary to say a little of Scientific Management in a more general fashion. I shall make no attempt to deal with the subject as a whole, because that would take me much too far afield from the subject of this book. I desire, however, to offer a few general observations which may serve to bring home some of the points made indirectly in the last chapter. I shall have little to say of those matters which fall under the head of Scientific Management while they do not directly and immediately affect the human element in the factory.

That the application of scientific principles to industrial organisation is a good thing we can all agree in the abstract; and we can at least reach an agreement in practice where only inanimate objects are affected. The improvement of industrial research, of factory organisation, of the estimating of costs of production, of the routing of jobs, of the dovetailing of orders, and of the co-ordination between shop and shop and between factory and factory undoubtedly call for more "science," and there can be no quarrel with any attempt to apply science purely in such spheres. There is a real sense in which industrial management is a science, just as there is a real sense in which political government is a science.

The advocates of the various systems which go by the name of Scientific Management make, however, a far wider claim than this. For Mr. Taylor, who invented the name if not the thing, the place of "science" in industrial management is not merely important, but all-embracing. His aim, at least, was to substitute in industry "the government of fact and law for the rule of force and opinion." He conceived industrial management not merely as a science, but as an exact science, furnishing an absolute and unchallengeable answer to every question, laying down natural laws with reference not simply to the machinery of the factory, but also to the behaviour, motions, tasks, and methods of remuneration of all the workers employed in it. He claimed that his system was "democratic," not because it established the principle of self-government by the workers in the factory, but because it made government an absolute and exact science, no less independent of the actual managers of any particular factory than of the workers employed in it.

The extreme claims of Mr. Taylor have been considerably modified by his theoretical successors, and very much more modified wherever Scientific Management has been applied in practice. Nevertheless, in so far as Scientific Management is a doctrine at all, it does rest upon the belief that industrial organisation is an exact science, and that in the factory the government of " natural law " must replace the rule of force and opinion.

This view is, of course, highly controversial, and, despite Mr. Taylor's elaborate promises of the beneficent effects which his system would have upon the workers, it is, I think, a theory which Labour is not likely to accept. The central point at issue can most easily be made clear by an analogy. We are all familiar with disputes concerning the place of the expert in political government. From time to time writers have arisen who have proclaimed that the government of men is an exact science, and that its basis and application should be determined by law and not by opinion. In all ages, from Plato to that talented French publicist, M. Émile Faguet, in our own day, such writers have challenged democracy as the denial of political science and as the " cult of incompetence." For the " inexact " and " unscientific " opinion of democracy they have desired to substitute the rule of knowledge by placing the expert in the seat of power. Against them, democrats have contended that, while the expert and science have their place in government, the social life of man is finally not a matter of abstract science, but a matter of positive will. They have based their conception of society upon the will of the governed, and have made the realisation of self-government their primary objective.

I do not think the advocates of Scientific Management in industry really believe in political democracy ; but they are, as a rule, careful to maintain that there is no analogy between industry and politics. Democracy in the sense of self-government, they say, may be good enough in politics, but it will not do in industry. Whatever politics may be, they hold that industrial management is an exact science.

This point of view I challenge. I hold firmly that no sphere of human action or conduct can be reduced to the formulae of an exact science. I hold that political self-government is good, not simply as ministering to " efficiency," but because it is self-government : and I hold that in every sphere of human action self-government is in itself good, because the greatest of man's achievements is the government of himself. I set out, then, from a fundamental criticism of the whole principle on which Scientific Management rests, and with an assertion that self-government is good in industry as well as in politics.

This is no denial that the expert has a place—and an important place—in industry; but it is a denial that the expert can be regarded as supreme. No less than in politics, the problem of democracy in industry is that of reconciling its own rule with an adequate recognition of the expert; but my point is that this is a problem for democracy to solve, and cannot be made a point against democracy itself.

I have primarily in mind the principle of industrial democracy, and I regard as the weightiest of arguments against any system the fact that it makes against self-government. I assume that our ideal in industry should be that of securing self-government for the workers engaged in it; and I am not interested in arguing with those who decisively reject this principle. "Humanitarian" arguments, based upon the effect of Scientific Management upon the "welfare" of the workers, may be important, but they are secondary.

I cannot attempt to define Scientific Management in any more concrete terms than I have employed in speaking of the general principle behind it. As soon as we pass from its theoretical position to the practical applications of that principle, we are confronted with a vast and heterogeneous mass of proposals. From these I must merely select those with which I propose to deal. In its application to Labour, Scientific Management is based upon a "scientific" investigation of the conditions under which work is carried on. By elaborate studies of the time taken on particular jobs or parts of jobs, the Scientific Manager seeks, as we have seen, to arrive at an accurate knowledge of the "best" conditions to be adopted in his factory. He seeks to equip himself with information in respect of every job bearing on the following, among other points:

(*a*) The method and amount of payment necessary to secure the lowest labour cost per unit of the product;

(*b*) The method of production, the hours and conditions of labour, the rest pauses, the amount of supervision, etc., necessary to secure the same ends.

This description of the methods and aims of Scientific Management includes what many of its advocates will regard as a misrepresentation. Our object, they will say, is not fundamentally that of securing "the lowest labour cost per unit of the product"; it is that of finding the "best" and "most scientific" methods of payment, hours and conditions of labour, rest pauses, amount of supervision, methods of production, etc. It is the fundamental doctrine at least of Mr. Taylor that these things go together. The "best" and most scientific adjustments do also secure the lowest labour costs, and also make for the common advantage of all parties concerned—the profiteer, the manager, the worker, and the public.

For this claim we should not, I think, be prepared to take Mr. Taylor's word, even if those who have to apply Scientific Management in practice were purely disinterested persons. Still less can we be content to do so when we consider the conditions under which the system has to be applied. Industry to-day is owned and controlled by persons who are not, and cannot be, "in business for their health." Self-interest and, failing that, competition, impel them to seek the lowest labour cost without too much regard for the effect upon others. Where it pays them to manage "scientifically," they will do so if they have the intelligence; where it does not pay them, or they are unintelligent, they will persist with unscientific management. If all managers were perfectly intelligent, and further if Scientific Management always paid its promoters, it would no doubt be universally adopted; but this would be no proof of its beneficent effect upon the workers or the community. The "best" for Capitalism is not necessarily the best for Labour or the best for the community. Indeed, in practice, the capitalist's criterion of what is "best" lies in the profit he can secure from it. This does not mean that it is necessarily bad for labour; but it does not mean either that it is necessarily good.

In addition to time-study and motion-study Scientific Management systems usually involve a considerable change in methods of workshop organisation. They have the effect of diminishing the power of the ordinary foreman, and sometimes in substituting for him, but more often in adding to him, a number of specialist experts whose business it is to apply scientific methods in certain definite spheres. In America studies of Scientific Management always dwell very largely upon what they call "the functional foreman," by which they mean an expert who has made a particular study of some one aspect of workshop organisation, and who is then employed to see that scientific methods are adopted throughout the factory in regard to his own particular class of work. Thus, there will be in an American "scientifically managed" concern special men who are motion-study experts, and other time-study experts, and others with functions which fall outside the immediate subject which we are considering. In Great Britain the principle of specialisation has not usually been so far developed, but a "scientifically managed" factory in this country will probably have installed an "Efficiency Engineer" and special "Time-Study Department" whose job it is to undertake both the fixing of times and prices, and the issuing of detailed instructions with regard to the methods of doing each job which is "scientifically managed." This naturally results in the transference of a good deal of power previously exercised in the workshop by the foreman to the Office and its expert staff, with the result that it may become more difficult for the workers in the workshop to assume any effective control, because bargaining about prices and times is removed to a sphere more distant from them, and more intimately a part of the business management of the concern. In fact, the Scientific Management shop tends to develop a new form of supervision which is not necessarily more harsh to the workers than the old-fashioned foreman, but which is certainly less closely in touch with the workers, and belongs to a much more distinct social caste.

A series of articles published two years ago in *Engineering*, and subsequently reprinted in book form,[1] included a most interesting section on "The Foreman of the Future," which, without specifically mentioning Scientific Management, brought this point of the growing distinction between the supervisors and the workers into considerable prominence. In the view of the writer of the articles it was desirable that the foreman of the future should belong to a social caste as distinct as possible from that of the workers, presumably in order to counteract any tendency that might otherwise manifest itself for foreman and workers to make common cause. It is a significant fact that during the war there was a marked tendency in this direction, and it is to be presumed that one of the "advantages" of Scientific Management from the point of view of some employers is that it would serve to counteract this tendency.

It is upon the fundamentally undemocratic character of Scientific Management in many of its aspects that attention ought to be specially concentrated. This point is somewhat obscured by the fact that discussion about it tends to be concentrated almost exclusively on questions of wage-payment, and so-called "scientific" systems for increasing output. In the last chapter I endeavoured to present a fair account of the principal characteristics of the most important of these systems; here I am concerned with a point which was only touched on in that connection.

We have seen that the worker is apt to judge "scientific" systems of payment purely by the amount which they enable him to earn. In so far as this is the case, the gradual fall in the piece-rate which is characteristic of such systems is concealed, and the worker is unaware that his extra effort is a source of more than proportionate profit to the employer. He may be making more money: and that is, *prima facie*, an argument in favour of the system.

Scientific Managers have nearly always encountered opposition on the part of the workers when they have attempted to introduce their systems. But it is notorious that, when once men have got used to a thing, they are far more ready to put up with it. The innovator's main difficulty is to get his scheme fairly launched without a stoppage; once it is established, he has a fair hope of keeping it in existence, even if it is unpopular. He is therefore willing to make concessions at the start, in order to make the scheme "go." Now, it is clear that, in all the systems we have described, the actual earnings of the workers depend upon the point at which the standard task of Taylor and Gantt, the 100 per cent efficiency of Harrington Emerson, and the standard time allowance of the Premium Bonus System are fixed. Fix them liberally, and high earnings will follow; illiberally, and earnings will be low.

[1] *The Man Power of the Nation* (*Engineering*, 1s.).

Here again there is a flaw in the "scientific" character of Scientific Management. Time- and motion-study do not and cannot decide whether the standard ought to be set on the basis of the superior worker or the ordinary worker, or on an average struck to cover all workers. They may suggest, after experiment, which method is most profitable to the employer: but they cannot easily prove this, and they certainly do not show which is the best method for the community.

The whole range of machine operations can be divided very broadly into two classes—repetition work and individual work. On repetition work the operative sticks to a narrow round of operations and produces constantly a more or less uniform product. On individual or jobbing work, on the other hand, the worker has usually a wider range of operations to perform, and the product varies from day to day or from week to week, both in character and in amount. It is clearly far easier to fix a standard of output and a constant price on repetition work than on jobbing work. No matter how great the number of operations performed may be, if they are of a recurring character, a standard price can with a fair chance of success be fixed for them. The cotton industry, with its elaborate weaving price-lists, affords the best example of this; but the method of the weavers' list could easily be applied over a far larger range of industries than now to jobs which are measurable in terms of output.

The measurement of individual or jobbing work is a far more complicated matter. Work of this class is usually far more skilled than repetition work, and, as the product varies continually, it is far more difficult to fix a standard price. Nevertheless, great efforts have been made by Scientific Managers and, in this country, by advocates of the Premium Bonus System, to apply their method to the widest possible range of skilled jobbing work. So far as the Premium Bonus System in this country is concerned, the result has very often been the fixing of basis times which have no sort of scientific sanction, in much the same haphazard way as piece prices are habitually fixed.

Here and there, however, there are cases in which the method of time- and motion-study has been carefully applied to jobbing as well as to repetition work. The result in such cases is often something like this. There is an enormous difference between skilled men in their ways of doing the same job, and this difference of method is clearly a constant attribute of skill. The first tendency of the Scientific Manager, as we have already seen, is to prescribe in detail to the skilled man how he shall do his work—what tools he shall use, and how he shall use them. A second tendency follows inevitably. On many classes of work subdivision is accomplished, and a large part of the work is taken away from the skilled man, and passes into the category of semi-skilled or unskilled work. And, of course, when such a change takes place, the employer claims to pay for the less skilled part of the job at a lower rate. This tendency has been very manifest during the war period, and many of the most difficult disputes have arisen over it.

The tendency, then, of Scientific Management is not simply in the direction of " scientific " systems of payment, but also in that of standardisation and the elimination of skill. In the storm centre, the engineering industry, its effect is to increase the amount of skilled labour required for the tool-room, while more than proportionately decreasing the skilled labour in the machine shops. In face of this tendency, which is no doubt largely inevitable, but which the war has greatly accelerated, the skilled mechanic sees himself threatened with the loss of his livelihood. The Scientific Manager replies that the increase of output made possible by the new methods will create so large a new demand as to absorb all the skilled labour. Even if this were true in the long run, it could hardly be expected to satisfy the skilled workman, whose economic position does not enable him to think in terms of the distant future.

There is a further tendency which arises directly out of those which we have just described. Standardisation takes the form not only of subdivision of labour within a works, but also, and increasingly, of the specialisation of works. The specialised shop or works, concentrating upon a single type of product, has long been established in America, and is now making great headway here. It is likely to make more headway in the future ; for it is clear that many big manufacturers have settled that the best results in mass-production are likely to be secured by specialised shops linked together within a single business unit.

This brings us to a further point. The general engineering shop, in which the proportion of individual work is high, is usually making mainly for special orders, and only to a small extent for stock. The specialised shop, on the other hand, which concentrates on repetition work, makes mainly for stock. During the war the existence of an unlimited demand did, of course, produce over all industry the conditions of making for stock.

One of the most frequent complaints by workmen against "scientific" systems is that, by increasing the output per worker, they create unemployment. It is the opinion of many investigators of the system that the effects in this respect differ in degree in specialised and general shops. In the general shop a system of strong inducements to a big hourly or daily output does produce unemployment, because it prevents the " nursing of work " and causes men to crowd the greatest possible output into one day or week, even if they have to stand off the next. These conditions exist also in the specialised shop, but not in the same degree, because it is possible for a shop that is making for stock to preserve a more regular level of output.

It is not, I think, generally realised what an enormous proportion of the unemployment in many industries really consists in "standing off" for a few days or weeks. This temporary unemployment is the worker's curse; for it means that he bears the burden out of his wages of maintaining himself during slackness of work as part of the employer's reserve of labour. The adoption of "scientific" systems of payment, which give the worker an inducement to "go all out" irrespective of the volume of work available, undoubtedly tends to increase the amount of temporary unemployment, and this is one of the most serious criticisms that can be levelled against it—a criticism which could only be surmounted by placing the whole burden of such unemployment upon the industry itself.

Economists and employers are very apt to scout the idea that there is any truth in the workmen's claim that "scientific" systems of inducement to output produce unemployment: but I think the above paragraphs show clearly one point wherein the workmen's contention is true.

Out of the facts surveyed in this and in the preceding chapter I can now proceed to draw together the threads of a conclusion.

In the first place, there is no essential or necessary connection between the application of scientific principles to industry and the adoption of fancy systems of payment which are unintelligible to the ordinary workman. These systems are uniformly false to their own premises, in that they do not provide for remuneration according to output or effort. They are not "scientific," (1) because science cannot determine the amount of payment that ought to be made; (2) because science cannot show whether the standard should be based on the exceptional, the average, or the ordinary worker; and (3) because their effect in respect of earnings depends upon the arbitrary fixing of a standard by the management, or by bargaining between the management and the workers. They are perhaps less unjust in their application to repetition than to jobbing work, but they are also in most cases less necessary, because the more automatic the machine, the less control, generally speaking, has the worker over his or her output. They are fundamentally unjust in their application to jobbing work, because on much work of such a class it is impossible to set an absolute and invariable standard, and also because the conditions under which such work has to be performed often differ widely from job to job. In short, they are fundamentally unscientific, unless the science in question is purely the science of unrestrained profiteering.

Time-work on some jobs, and piece-work with a guaranteed weekly rate on others, afford all the inducements to output which ought to be afforded; and the decision on any class of work as between time-work and piece-work ought to be made by negotiation between the employers and the Trade Unions on the merits of each case. Where piece-work is adopted, more scientific systems of determining piece-work prices ought to be devised: but the determination ought to be made jointly by the two sides, and the science necessary for it ought to be in the possession of both.

This brings me to my second point. Time-study, motion-study, and the other expedients of Scientific Management may have some beneficent results, especially in such spheres as the study of industrial fatigue and the relation of output to hours of labour. But here again science must not be the monopoly of the management or of the employer. The Trade Unions must equip themselves with the knowledge that is required, and "science" must become the handmaid of collective bargaining. Just as it is one thing to say that "welfare" is desirable, and quite another to approve of "welfare work" under the employer's control, so it is one thing to desire industry to become more scientific, and quite another to accept Scientific Management at the hands of the employing class. Taylor's contention that under such conditions an equal balance will be struck between the management and the workers, because both will be subject to the "rule of law," is unmitigated nonsense.

Thirdly, Scientific Management presents a number of real dangers to industrial democracy. The methods of payment which it suggests are for the most part a crude appeal to individualism, and it is generally agreed among Trade Unionists that where they are adopted the *moral* and sense of solidarity among the workers are often lowered. They tend to set each man's hand against the others, and inaugurate a system of cut-throat competition between worker and worker, even in the same grade. In many of their applications they may be fatal to collective bargaining and the standard rate, though this is not necessarily or universally true of all parts or aspects of them. It is most true where Scientific Managers adopt the device of a "scientific" grading of labour which subdivides the workers into very small groups, or even treats each worker individually on his merits. Against such tendencies Trade Unionism must fight. It must preserve at all costs its effective right of collective bargaining, the standard rate, and the solidarity of Labour.

Fourthly, Scientific Management tends to make more impassable the gulf between Labour and Management. This is an aspect which I have already referred to in dealing with the "functional foreman." In place of promotion from the ranks of the workers Scientific Management would find its foremen by special selection, and train them largely away from the workshop. In this way the foremen would come to have less of the Labour and more of the employer's point of view, and would become, far more than now, a new class of dependents on Capitalism. For one who believes, like myself, that one of the next steps for Trade Unionism, in its gradual assumption of control over industry, will be to take altogether out of the employers' hands and vest in the Trade Union the appointment of foremen and the organisation of the workshop, this appears as a counter-move on the part of Capitalism to remove the foremen from the possibility of control by Labour. The way for Labour, to my thinking, is the gradual conquest of management. For this, Labour must equip itself with scientific and industrial knowledge; and, while it is doing so, it must resist any move by the employing class which will make more difficult the conquest of industrial control.

This is one reason why there can be no question, on the ground of their effect on output, of scrapping Trade Union rules. These rules are the beginnings of democratic industrial legislation. They are resented by the employers as invasions of capitalist autocracy, and as outrages upon capitalistic "competence." The employer, on his own showing, knows how to run industry: the workman does not. If that is so, I reply that the workman must learn, and that the best way for him to do so is for him to increase his control. Let Trade Union rules be improved, by all means: but they must be improved by the Trade Unions. They must be upheld because they point the way to industrial self-government.

My fifth point follows logically. The employer, I have said, on his own showing, knows how to run industry. Does he? It would seem that during the war he has been discovering very rapidly that he does not, if we can judge from the cry for reorganisation which has arisen in the employers' own ranks. There is a very wide scope indeed for scientific reorganisation of industrial methods: and if the employers would devote to these half the attention which they devote to trying to bully, badger, bribe, or cajole Labour into the acceptance of unscientific systems of payment by results, it would be better for all concerned. The biggest and most natural field for science in industry is in the management of inanimate objects; and there let it be applied to the full. Where it affects men, and is applied to men, its effects are far more problematical.

Sixthly, we have seen that the workers are very largely justified in their belief that, in many cases, scientific systems may create unemployment by creating conditions under which temporary unemployment is profitable to the employer. If this is to be counteracted, it should surely be done by placing the burden of unemployment, not upon the State, but upon the industry concerned. Let the employers be compelled by the State to pay to the Unions a maintenance allowance for all members affected by such unemployment, and one motive for the offering of unscientific inducements to Labour will disappear and in addition a big step will have been taken in the direction of decasualisation.

Scientific Management contains many good features to which no objection can be taken; but its claim to be a water-tight and complete scientific system for industry is as false as its claim to be democratic. Our problem in industry is the creation of an efficient and democratic system. We must apply science; but we must not allow science to be a class monopoly. The Trade Unions must train themselves for control; and, in doing so, they must resist all changes which would have the effect of destroying or weakening their economic power. They must not, for their own sakes, block all industrial change; but they must adapt it to their needs as well as themselves to it. We cannot expect a truly efficient system in industry until we have an enlightened democracy capable of controlling industry; we cannot abolish the class-struggle with a blast from the trumpet of science. But we can make up our minds that the end towards which we must strive is industrial self-government: and we can test the schemes of Scientific Management by means of this principle. If we do this, we shall not find it wholly bad; but we shall find in it many dangers against which Labour must be on its guard.

CHAPTER IX

THE SPHERE OF PRICE LISTS

The survey which we have given in earlier chapters of this book of the various systems of payment by results should at least have served to bring home to the reader at once the complexity of the subject and the difficulties which stand in the way of a satisfactory treatment of it from the worker's point of view. We have referred again and again in passing to the problem of collective bargaining in the fixing and adjustment of piece-work prices and standard time allowances, and we have seen more than once what is in reality the crux of the immediate problem. We have now to confront these difficulties more directly, and to discuss the ways in which collective bargaining can best be applied where systems of payment by results are allowed to operate.

The rest of this book will inevitably be of a more controversial character than most of what has gone before. Except, perhaps, in the last chapter, we have so far mainly described the various systems with the minimum of comment upon them, except in relation to incidental points. We have now to suggest ways of handling the problem from the Trade Union point of view. There is room for considerable difference of opinion with regard to most of the suggestions put forward, and it will be found that different trades, and even the same trades in different districts, take up very varying attitudes towards the proper method of dealing with questions of payment by results. It is, however, possible from the experience which the Trade Union movement has gained in handling the problem, both from its successes and its failures, to learn certain lessons which may be of advantage in dealing with it in the future.

It will be most convenient to deal first with those trades and industries in which the predominant method of payment by results admits of the fullest amount of collective bargaining by Employers' Associations and Trade Unions; that is to say, in which the system of the standard list of prices has been most fully developed. As we saw in the second chapter of this book, price lists have been adopted over a considerable range of industry, especially in those occupations in which a given effort can be most nearly relied upon to produce a given output, and in which there is an easy method of calculating output in terms of some definite unit, such as the ton, or the yard, or the number of articles on pure repetition jobs.

The industry in which price lists have been most fully and perfectly developed is undoubtedly the cotton industry, where the standard price lists of the weavers, and to a less extent of the spinners, have stood the test of long years of experience, and have proved on the whole a satisfactory method of wage-payment. The output of the cotton industry is standardised, and it is therefore possible to set out in elaborate detail the prices to be paid for practically all the operations that have to be performed. This does not mean that the number of operations is small, or that there is not a very wide variety in the classes of goods produced. It means only that the whole, or nearly the whole, of this very wide variety can be reduced to comparatively simple elements. Indeed, the weavers' list is, to the outsider, one of the most complicated documents in existence, and one which is completely unintelligible to those who are not experts at the trade. Nevertheless, given the necessary expert knowledge, the computing of the price to be paid for any particular operation is in most cases merely a matter of mathematics. The calculations involved are often exceedingly complicated, and require the taking into account of a very large number of different factors, so that the list itself is long and contains many complicated elements. It is, however, possible, with the list as basis, to fix the price for any operation with the nearest approximation to mathematical certainty that any industry is likely to attain.

At one time there were no standard lists for cotton weaving, and prices were fixed mill by mill, either by the employer acting on his own, or by the most rudimentary principles of collective bargaining. Subsequently district lists came into force in all the organised districts, and more recently these district lists gave place to a uniform list which is now in general use in North and North-East Lancashire, and often forms the basis on which prices are fixed even in those centres which do not directly adopt it in its entirety. The uniform list which applies to nearly the whole industry deals directly only with what are called "plain goods," but the manufacture of other and more special types of cloth is also regulated indirectly by the list, the necessary modifications being made in order to adapt the list to their special conditions. It is not possible here to give an intelligible account of the method adopted in the cotton weavers' list without devoting an entirely undue amount of space to the subject. Our only point here is to stress the fact that in the complicated operations of this particular industry, standardisation of machinery and product has made it possible almost entirely to eliminate detailed bargaining with regard to particular operations, and to fix all prices on a uniform principle depending upon a collective agreement between the Weavers'

Amalgamation and the National Federation of Cotton Spinners and Manufacturers.[1]

Cotton-spinning is not regulated by a universal list applicable to all districts. There are, however, two lists for Oldham and Bolton respectively, each of which has been adopted over a considerable area ; so that, on the whole, the methods of fixing prices for cotton-spinning are the subject of collective agreements almost as comprehensive and water-tight as those of the weavers. Certain other branches of the cotton industry are regulated by very similar lists, either local or national in character. There are, for instance, special lists for velvet weaving, warp dressing, twisting, and drawing, and other operations. In fact, it may be said in general that practically the whole cotton industry of Lancashire and the adjoining counties is fully regulated so far as piece-work prices are concerned, by agreed price lists of very wide application.

This method of regulation has involved the calling into existence of a highly specialised class of Trade Union officials, equipped with the technical knowledge which is necessary for dealing with problems arising out of the lists. How far the method adopted in the cotton industry, by which a Trade Union official possessing these special qualifications is also in charge of the organising work of the Trade Union, is a good one is open to doubt, since it seems probable that different qualities are desirable in an official who is primarily an organiser and in one who is primarily an expert. To this problem we shall have to return at a later stage.

It is probable that the elaborate methods of price regulation which have been applied so successfully in the cotton industry are applicable no less to the other branches of textile work. So far, however, the other textile industries have not been anything like so completely covered by standard lists. The industry that stands next in importance is the woollen and worsted industry, and in this, although lists exist, they are mostly local in character, and are for the most part nothing like so elaborate or comprehensive as the standard lists which prevail in the cotton industry.[2] It has long been recognised that one of the main problems confronting Trade Unionism in the woollen industry is the establishing of universal lists of the type which prevails throughout the whole of the cotton industry.

Hosiery, lace, silk, carpets, elastic web, and other branches of textiles have also lists of local application which follow in the main the same principles as those prevailing in the cotton industry.[2]

It has been possible to apply the principle of the standard price

[1] A sufficiently full explanation of the cotton weaving lists and also of the lists prevailing in the other branches of the cotton industry will be found in the *Report on Collective Agreements* published by the Board of Trade Labour Department, 1910 (C.D. 5366), price 2s. 2d.

[2] See *Collective Agreements*, as above.

list so widely over the textile industries, despite the enormous variety of the types of cloth, etc., produced, because in practically all cases the operations necessary for producing these varieties can be reduced to standard elements. These standard elements being priced, the price to be paid for each variety of product follows almost as a matter of course. It is not, of course, suggested that the element of error can be totally eliminated; but it has at least been reduced to such small proportions that there is at present no really important problem outstanding for solution.[1] This does not mean that wages in the cotton industry or in any other textile industry are satisfactory; it only means that, assuming a standard of living, the problem of adjusting piece-work prices to this standard has been largely solved. In fact, when wages are increased or reduced in the textile industries, the usual method is not to alter the list, but to add or deduct a certain percentage on or off all piece-work prices. The list thus remains in being irrespective of actual fluctuations in the rate of wages.

In the boot and shoe industry the principle of the standard list has been fairly widely applied, and is in operation wherever any system of payment by results is worked by men, though in a large number of cases women are still deprived of the protection of a standard list. In this case, again, there is a wide variety in product; but, however many different styles of boots and shoes may be produced, the work necessary for their production, so far as machine-made products are concerned, can be reduced mainly to standard elements, and therefore in these cases, again, variety in the product presents no obstacles to a standard list. The boot and shoe lists are in all cases local in character, but the methods adopted in drawing up "the piece-work statements" for various districts are largely uniform, and are based upon and principally determined by national agreements between the employers and the National Union of Boot and Shoe Operatives.[2] Lists exist in certain cases for hand-work as well as for machine-work; but in hand-work the lists naturally admit of a much larger margin of error than in the case of machine operations in which the time is largely determined by the machine itself.

A quite different aspect of price lists is represented by the mining industry. As we have seen in an earlier chapter, coal-getting is in all districts for the most part a piece-work operation, and in some districts a considerable amount of other work, including the putting up of pit props, haulage, and various other types of work, is also paid on a piece-work system. This is especially the case in South Wales, where every possible type of work is on a piece-work basis, even surface haulage being paid in some cases on a collective tonnage basis. In other districts, as in Durham, the

1 Except that arising from defective material. See Chapter II. page 13.

2 The Amalgamated Union of Co-operative Employees has also recently drawn up a standard list of prices for boot-repairers in co-operative shops.

greater part of the work, apart from actual coal-getting, is paid for on day-work rates.

Usually the price lists which prevail in the mining industry are "pit" lists, or rather "seam" lists, that is to say, a separate list of prices is prepared for each pit or even for each seam in a large pit. These price lists cover tonnage rates for various classes of coal, together with the rates, by time or piece, to be paid for operations other than coal-getting. A short extract from a typical South Wales list will serve to illustrate their general character.[1]

The method of the pit list, however, is not universally applied over the whole mining industry. Durham and some other districts work on the County Average System, *i.e.* a standard list of average earnings for each class of workers is fixed by negotiation for the whole county, and the prices to be paid in particular collieries or in particular seams are fixed by local negotiation through a Joint Committee on the basis of the county average rate. This universal list for the whole coalfield is thus not the actual basis of payment in all collieries. The method adopted is that of taking certain typical collieries as the standard, and ascertaining the average earnings in these collieries. This average thus becomes the standard, and when prices to be paid at any other colliery come under consideration the standard list is used as the starting-point for bargaining, and the miners' officials agree with the coal-owners' representatives on what is regarded as a fair addition to, or subtraction from, the prices, in accordance with the particular character of each mine, difficulty of work, thickness of seams, etc. In South Wales, Derbyshire, and other districts, on the other hand, a separate agreed list is made for each colliery, and in South Wales, at least, a list once fixed is never altered. The bargaining over such lists is one of the main activities of the South Wales Miners' Federation. The men try, as a rule without success, to get a list fixed before the pit or seam is opened; the owners try to delay a settlement until they know how the seams are turning out. Cases that cannot be settled at the pit are referred to the Conciliation Board.

In some parts of Scotland an intermediate system exists. In Lanarkshire there is no uniform list for the whole county, but collieries are, in a number of cases, arranged in groups, and a price list is fixed, not for an individual colliery, but for a group of associated collieries.

There is much division of opinion with regard to the respective merits of these various systems of fixing wages. The Durham miners usually uphold their method of the standard list, while miners in some other districts have endeavoured to secure similar lists, so far without success. On the other hand, the South Wales miners usually scout the possibility of such a standard list in their own coalfield. They hold that pits differ so widely one from another that no grouping or averaging is practicable in their case. It seems

[1] See Appendix F (*i*), p. 141.

probable that, in fact, the difference in the conditions of coal-getting, as between one area and another, necessitates different methods of piece-work payment ; but of this question we shall have something further to say in a later part of this chapter.

The system adopted by the Boilermakers' Society in the shipyards resembles in some ways the Durham County Average System. The members of this society mostly work piece-work, except on certain classes of repair work. In the case of the riveting squads the basis of payment is collective, the holders-up receiving a fixed proportion of the earnings of the riveters. Helpers, who are organised in the National Amalgamated Union of Labour, are paid at time-rates. Piece-work prices are fixed for districts and incorporated in printed lists, showing the standard prices for a very wide range of jobs. The Tyne and Wear list, for instance, runs to forty-six closely printed pages. Variations in rates of wages subsequent to the compilation of the standard list are calculated in percentages on or off the printed list, according to the nature of the job and the mechanical equipment of the yard. The lists include not only normal piece-work prices, but also special allowances on difficult, onerous, or unpleasant jobs. No bonus systems are worked in the trade, the Union, which is practically blackleg-proof, not recognising them. Negotiations dealing with piece-work prices (*i.e.* percentages on or off the standard lists) are complicated and constant. They are conducted by the full-time District Delegates whom the society maintains in the principal centres. It will be seen that the trade is one in which piece-work has been completely reconciled with collective bargaining, the individual workman having practically no share in fixing the price, which is fixed for him by direct bargaining between the Union and the employers.

Among the shipwrights time-work has hitherto prevailed, although piece-work has been introduced to a considerable extent during the war. The only section which habitually worked piece-work before the war was the drillers, and in their case the conditions are almost exactly the same as those applying to boilermakers, except that the printed lists more often refer to particular yards, and that there is a range of jobs for which prices are fixed by individual bargain, with an appeal to collective bargaining where necessary. The price lists are somewhat less complicated than those of the boilermakers.

It is not necessary here to go in more detail into the question of price lists, since this chapter is not intended as an exhaustive enumeration of price-list systems, but merely as a general indication of the scope and character of such lists. Before we leave the subject, however, we must endeavour to point more clearly to the factors which make for and against the successful operation of the price list in industry generally. We have already seen that the price-list system can be applied only where there is some more or less uniform method of measuring output in terms of some constant unit. Naturally, the degree in which this unit really affords a satisfactory method on which to base wage-payments depends on the extent to which the conditions of production are uniform from one operation to another. Here the first problem that confronts us is that of the material used. Again and again it is found that, even where price lists of the most scientific character exist, difficulty arises because there is not absolute uniformity in the material that has to be worked upon. Thus, the spinner complains of bad cotton, the weaver of faulty yarn, the turner of defective castings, the wood-worker of a flaw in the wood upon which he is asked to work, or still more often, of bad weathering, or other defects due to climatic conditions. It is difficult to secure, in most cases, a sufficient uniformity in the material used to be quite sure that the element of variation in the output secured by a given amount of effort is totally eliminated. Bad spinning controversies are continually arising throughout the cotton industry, and similar controversies exist in connection with most price-list systems on machine-work.

The second problem is that of the machine itself. Even if the material is absolutely uniform and without flaw, the machine may be old, or out of order, or for some other reason may not work smoothly and well. In almost all cases some special provision has to be made in a piece-work system for falling off in piece-work earnings, on account of stoppages or defects in machinery, and this element may in some cases rise to startling proportions.

Moreover, in a good number of trades, and more especially in general engineering, the same job has to be done on different occasions on different machines. These different machines may not all be exactly suited to the job. For instance, a job which can be done on one machine without any special adjustments of jigs, tools, etc., may, on another machine, require the spending of a considerable time in rigging up adjustments, and even when this has been done the machine may not be able to do the work as quickly as the other type. It may require, for instance, a greater number of cuts to secure the same result. If two workmen working on two different machines of different capacity for the job are paid at the same piece-work price, clearly the same amount of effort on the part of both will not produce the same earnings. This is, indeed, one of the most serious objections to the application of any price list to such an industry as general engineering.

Nor is the problem always one of the particular machine on which the man who is doing the job is working. It is also a problem of the supply of power in the shop, and of the relation of one machine to another. A fault in the power-station, or a partial breakdown, may delay all work, and give rise to the necessity of making still further allowances.

Again, on many classes of work output depends, not on the individual effort of one worker, or on the nature of the material on which that individual is working, or on the machine on which he is working alone, but on the co-ordination between a whole group of workers engaged on consecutive operations which form part of a single job. In such cases it may be possible to secure a remuneration corresponding roughly to group effort by the adoption of a collective system of payment ; but an individual system of payment by results applied to such group or team work is almost inevitably unjust and capricious in its working.

These problems have been described in their relation more particularly to machine operations. Similar difficulties, however, exist equally, if not more, on many types of hand-work. For instance, in the mines the problem of the abnormal place is often more acute than the problem of bad material or defective machinery in cotton or engineering. An abnormal place means a place in which the miner, by putting forth his average effort, cannot secure a fair return measured in tonnage produced. It was largely to meet the difficulty of such abnormal places that the miners pressed in the 1912 strike for minimum rates of wages for coal-hewers and other classes of workers, and the Coal Mines Minimum Wage Act of 1912, so far as hewers are concerned, is mainly operative in securing for the worker in an abnormal place at least a minimum rate of wages. It may be said that the abnormal place difficulty is not, in fact, as serious as it seems, because men shift round from place to place, and the good and bad places are therefore fairly averaged out. This, however, is by no means always the case. Favouritism and victimisation, as well as mere accident, may conspire to keep a man for long periods in a place in a pit in which he cannot earn a fair living wage. Even the Coal Mines Minimum Wage Act by no means suffices to correct the disparity, since it secures only a minimum rate which is, in fact, considerably below the average earnings of the pit. The abnormal place difficulty was probably very largely present in the minds of the Lancashire and Cheshire miners when they moved, at the Annual Conference of the Miners' Federation, for the abolition of all piece-work in the mines.[1]

The difficulty attaching to price lists is not confined to the problems which we have already described. A price list of necessity relates only to operations which are already in existence, and to methods of performing such operations which are already in vogue. Continually there are being introduced into industry new operations and new methods of performing old operations. There continually arises, therefore, the necessity for a revision of price lists, and for the addition of prices for new jobs. Where adequate machinery has been set up for the original formulation of the price list, there is no insuperable difficulty in keeping such machinery in being for the readjustment of lists as new difficulties arise. But in any important industry this readjustment is highly complicated, and necessitates almost day-to-day negotiation between the parties concerned. In the absence of effective machinery for day-to-day

[1] See Chapter II.

collective bargaining, a price list will not, however well it was originally designed, long continue to secure a fair correspondence of earnings to effort. On the other hand, the advantages of a price list, where payment by results is already in operation, are sufficiently obvious. The greatest defect of ordinary piece-work systems lies in the fact that it is the employer who fixes the piece-work price, and that his fixing is liable to be in the first place capricious, and in the second place unjust. It is obviously an advantage to get down in black and white an agreed list of prices covering a whole trade, or at least a whole district, or a whole workshop. An enormous amount of friction is saved by such a method; instead of being liable to quarrel every day over every price that is fixed, workmen and employers can only quarrel upon a firm basis of agreed prices. The need for bargaining does not disappear; but the amount of day-to-day work which it involves is greatly reduced. At least, the actual amount of work is reduced if previously bargaining has taken place on each piece-work price individually. More often this has not been the case, and the effect of the price list is not so much to reduce bargaining as to create order where chaos previously prevailed.

Just as there is an obvious advantage in securing a price list over any area, there is an equally obvious advantage in making it applicable over as wide an area as possible. A separate price list for each town in the cotton industry means many times as much effort spent over collective bargaining as a single price list applicable over a whole section of the industry. A national list, where the conditions are such as to make it possible, is obviously to be preferred to a purely local list. Even greater advantages would no doubt attach to an international price list, if such a list were possible at the present stage of international economic relationships.

Even without going to the length of any such Utopian speculations, we can see at once that there is plenty of room for the extension of price-list systems. The woollen industry, the smaller textile industries, and even many branches of the cotton industry are still without national lists; and if, in these chosen homes of the price-list system, the position still leaves so much to be desired, it is not surprising that the situation in other industries is very much more defective. There is an indefinite amount of room for the expansion of the price-list system, even in the opinion of those who do not believe that this system is applicable to the whole range of industry. But to this problem of the applicability of price lists to those industries in which work is largely not of a repetitive but of a jobbing character we shall have to return in the course of our discussion of the present methods of price-fixing which prevail in those industries, and more particularly in most of the metal trades.

CHAPTER X

"MUTUALITY" AND COLLECTIVE BARGAINING

We have seen that over a considerable range of industries piece-work is regulated by standard price lists, usually printed, applying nationally or to a particular locality, or to a particular workshop or group of workshops. We have now to deal with those trades and industries in which systems of payment by results are in operation without the protection afforded by any such printed lists of prices.

This is the case above all in the engineering and kindred trades, where various systems of payment by results were very widely in operation before the war, and have, during the war, been very considerably extended. The dominant method of price-fixing in the engineering industry is usually called "Mutuality." In the words of the engineering agreement of 1907 this means that "the prices to be paid shall be fixed by mutual arrangement between the employer and the workman or workmen who perform the work." That is to say, according to the theory of "mutuality," each workman (or group of workmen in the case of collective jobs) is left to make a separate bargain with the employer or his representative, the foreman or rate-fixer. As we saw in an earlier chapter, this provision that "mutuality" shall apply in the fixing of prices was incorporated by the Trade Unions in the dilution scheme under which women were introduced during the war, and also formed a clause of the well-known Circular L2, which covered the conditions of women's employment on men's work. "Mutuality" was fought for and won, in theory at least, by the Trade Unions in the skilled metal trades, and is regarded, or has, in the past, been regarded by them as an important Trade Union principle. It is taken by the skilled workman to mean that before he starts on a job on piece-work, a price for that job shall have been agreed upon between himself and the employer, and that he has the right to raise an objection to the price suggested by the employer, and not to start on the job until some arrangement has been come to, and either a new price fixed, or at least the promise of redress given.

In effect the system works very differently in well-organised shops and trades and in less organised shops and trades. A skilled workman in a well-organised shop may be, and often is, in a perfectly good position for driving a bargain with his employer or foreman on the question of the piece-work price to be paid, although it is easily possible to exaggerate the extent to which the system of "mutuality" works well, even in the best-organised shops. The conditions are obviously widely different where unskilled workers or women, with far less bargaining power behind them, work under a similar system; for in such cases the "mutuality" is often, in fact, all on the one side. The employer fixes the price, and the worker is practically compelled to accept it. Where this is the case "mutuality" is not a system of collective bargaining at all, but the absolute negation of collective bargaining, and a return to the system of pure individualism.

Let us then try to look at "mutuality" from the point of view of these two classes of workers separately. The skilled workman in the engineering trades is conscious that much of his work is not of a class to which a rigid price list can easily be applied. In normal times it is largely work of a jobbing character. That is to say, the number of different jobs is very great, and the number of times the same job has to be done usually small. There is thus practically no opportunity for a price list, since a price list would mean in effect, something very like fixing by collective bargaining a separate price for nearly every operation performed in the shop.

The skilled workman attains a very considerable knowledge and accuracy in the pricing of jobs. When a job is brought to him he can tell how long the job is likely to take, often far better than the salaried persons employed by the firm to fix prices. He is thus often in a good position for driving a bargain with his employer, and, from the point of view of the most highly skilled workman engaged on work of an individual character, there is no doubt that the system of "mutuality" works fairly satisfactorily. As soon, however, as there is any approach to repetitive work, that is to say, as soon as a large number of identical or similar jobs are being done in a shop, it is inevitable that the price paid for one job should be used as a precedent in fixing the price to be paid for future jobs. Where this is so, the price paid to any particular workman at once becomes a matter, not for the workman alone, but for the whole shop. If a single workman makes a bad bargain and accepts a low price on a particular job, he may well be injuring his fellows, because the same price is likely to be forced upon them, when that job, or one like it, has to be done again.

It will be found that in nearly all organised shops in which "mutuality" is in operation there is also a certain amount of common action by the men in the shop in the matter of prices. This co-operation may be only of the most rudimentary character. The men may merely discuss prices one with another, and get a rough idea in their minds of the level of prices that ought to be insisted upon; but in large and strongly organised shops the element of collective bargaining very often goes much further. The men regularly decide among themselves what are the prices that they are prepared to accept, and enforce these prices mutually on one another, and collectively upon the management. Sometimes a formal organisation is set up among the workers in the shop for the purpose of regulating prices, a Shop Committee being established, whose duty it is to keep a watch on the fixing and adjustment of all prices in the shop. Of such Committees we shall have a good deal more to say in the next chapter.

If " mutuality " is in some cases fairly satisfactory, and can in others be fairly easily modified so far as organised workers are concerned, it is entirely unsatisfactory in the case of less strongly organised workers engaged upon repetitive work. Where a number of workers are engaged upon the same job, the practice by which each worker is supposed to arrange separately with the management the price to be paid, is not a form, but a complete negation, of collective bargaining. There is, in fact, no possible doubt that, where payment by results is applied to repetitive jobs, the only tolerable method is that of the price list. This does not mean necessarily a national or district list; but it does mean, at the very least, a written list applicable to the whole shop, and arrived at by collective agreement between the Trade Union or Trade Unions concerned and the management. There would seem no reason in many cases why the area covered by such a list should not be considerably wider, or why national lists should not be applied to many branches of metal work, as they have been applied to textiles and to other industries.

The main reason why " mutuality " is so completely unsatisfactory when it is applied to unskilled workers is that individually the unskilled worker has practically no bargaining power. Without a system of collective bargaining, the unskilled worker is absolutely at the mercy of the employer in the matter of price-fixing. This is seen very clearly throughout the sweated and unorganised trades, more particularly wherever women are largely employed. Women, as a rule, outside the textile industry, tend to be employed on systems of payment by results without collective bargaining or price lists. It seems clear that this is fundamentally wrong, and that, where legislative regulation of wages takes place, as under the Trade Boards Act, Trade Boards should extend their action, not merely to the fixing or guaranteeing of minimum time-rates, but also to the fixing of minimum piece-work conditions applicable over the widest possible area.

Even " mutuality " is not the most unsatisfactory method at present prevailing in the metal trades. In theory, the employer does not even recognise " mutuality " in respect of the fixing of standard time allowances under the Premium Bonus System, or the various system of " output bonus." The theory, on the introduction of the Premium Bonus System, was that the bonus was an *ex gratia* allowance, that the day-work rate was guaranteed, and that over and above that rate the employer made a "little present" to the worker, if he was good and produced a lot of work. There was, then, on the employer's showing, no need for collective bargaining under the Premium Bonus System, and the Carlisle Memorandum of 1902, under which the Amalgamated Society of Engineers agreed to the introduction of the system, contains no reference to collective bargaining or even to "mutuality." Time-rates were to be guaranteed, and standard time allowances, once they had been established, were only to be changed if the method or means of manufacture was changed; but there the safeguards stopped. There was no provision at all for collective bargaining, and up to the present day the employers have never formally recognised collective bargaining under the bonus system.

In practice "mutuality" and the various modifications of "mutuality" have no doubt often prevailed, and, in the procedure now adopted under the agreement in connection with the adjustment of Premium Bonus basis times in the Barrow engineering trades, elaborate regulations are laid down for negotiation between the management and the men concerned. These regulations extend not simply to "mutuality," but also to a system of general consultation between the management and representatives of the trades concerned. Similar forms of procedure recognising "mutuality" and workshop bargaining have been adopted in other districts in which bonus systems are in operation; but it is still the case that there is no national recognition by the Employers' Federation of collective bargaining in connection with basis times. The matter of recognition of collective bargaining in such cases has come under discussion during the war period; but no final agreement on the question has so far been arrived at.

The method of "mutuality" is a dying method. As standardisation, subdivision of processes, and specialisation in all branches of industry increase, the area over which standard price lists can be put into operation grows continually wider. Moreover, even in the operations which continue to be of a non-repetitive character, it does not follow that the only available method of price-fixing is by "mutuality." There is the intermediate system of collective bargaining through some form of workshop organisation, backed by the power of the Trade Union. To possible developments in this method we must now turn our attention.

CHAPTER XI

WORKSHOP COMMITTEES AND WORKSHOP BARGAINING

One of the most significant developments in Trade Union machinery during the war period has been the growth of organisation inside the workshops, and the extension of the functions of such organisation to collective bargaining on "domestic" questions. For many years before the war there were, in large numbers of trades, workshop officials, in some cases recognised, in others unrecognised, by the Trade Unions, and called by various names: shop stewards, shop delegates, workshop representatives, yard committee men, etc. Moreover, in a good number of cases, these shop delegates had formed Workshop or Works Committees of a more or less stable and definite character; and in other cases Workshop or Works Committees more or less loosely attached to the Trade Unions had come into existence in one form or another. The oldest of all these forms of organisations is, of course, the Printers' Chapel, the organisation of the compositors in each Union printing-house, which dates back far beyond the beginnings of modern Trade Unionism in the printing industry.

We are here concerned with workshop and works organisation only in so far as it deals with problems of wage-payment. Some Works and Workshop Committees have no such functions at all. That is to say, they are practically confined to questions of welfare, social amenities, sports, etc., in the works, and do not deal in any way with Trade Union or industrial questions: others, while they deal with industrial questions to a certain extent, have no jurisdicdiction, recognised or unrecognised, over questions of wage-payment. Similarly with shop stewards and shop delegates, in some cases the shop delegate is merely the representative of the Union in the shop for the purpose of examining Trade Union cards, seeing that the new workmen introduced into the shop join a recognised Union, and that old members keep up their payments punctually. In other cases the shop delegate or shop steward has assumed important functions in relation to industrial matters, including the fixing, and still more the adjustment, of disputed piece-work prices. It is particularly in these directions that the development of workshop organisation during the war period has been noticeable.

The Printers' Chapel has long had functions fully recognised by the Printing Trade Unions in dealing with matters arising out of price lists, whether for time-work or for piece-work. The same may be said of shop delegates in many other trades, notably in bookbinding, and in certain branches of shipbuilding. In the engineering trades shop stewards have, as a rule, had no recognised functions in dealing with such questions; but in many cases, either shop stewards or Trade Union Workshop Committees of various kinds have actually exercised a good deal of power in this connection.

It is necessary here to distinguish clearly between two classes of problems which arise in relation to wage-payment. First, there is the problem of the general method of wage-payment that is to be adopted. For example, there is the question whether payment shall be by time or by results, and, if payment by results is adopted, the question what particular system is to be accepted under collective agreement. With such matters Workshop Committees have, under the constitution of most Trade Unions, no final authority to deal. In particular, the question whether payment by results is to be accepted or not has almost always to be referred for decision either by the national Executives of the Trade Unions concerned, or more often by their District Committees. Thus, no Workshop Committee, even if it were fully recognised by a Trade Union or group of Trade Unions in the engineering industry, would have any jurisdiction in decreeing the adoption of a system of payment by results unless it had received general sanction from the District Committees of the Trade Unions concerned.

If, however, a District Committee had agreed, in general terms, to the introduction of payment by results, negotiations concerning the particular system of payment to be adopted in a particular works or workshop might frequently be carried on through the Works Committee or Shop Stewards' Committee. In such cases the Works Committee would have no power, under the constitution of the Trade Unions, to reach a final settlement with the management, but would have constitutionally to submit any draft agreement arrived at for ratification by the District Committees concerned. In practice this rule is sometimes infringed, and this has been particularly so during the war period, while dilution has been in operation. There have been a number of complaints by Trade Unions that shop stewards and Works Committees have accepted systems of payment by results without waiting for ratification by the constitutional machinery of their Trade Unions. Such a practice obviously tends to break down the Trade Union principle that collective bargaining shall take place over the widest possible area, by introducing the possibility that a particular group of stewards or workmen will accept a system of payment by results which is contrary to the interests of their fellow-workmen in other shops, and perhaps to the general practice established by the District Committee in dealing with such questions.

From the above question of principle it is necessary to distinguish sharply particular applications of principles already laid down to individual jobs. Workshop Committees, where they are firmly established, have often considerably wider functions in relation to such questions. In speaking of " mutuality," we have stated that the pure principle of " mutuality " recognised under the Engineering Agreement tends, in fact, continually to be modified by the development of collective bargaining in the workshops. This collective bargaining is found in its most rudimentary form where the workman who is to perform a particular job, instead of agreeing individually upon a price with the foreman, takes along with him two or three of his fellow-workmen, and thus conducts with the foreman a more or less rudimentary collective bargain. It is not a long step from this practice to the constitution of a more or less definite Works Committee, which as a regular practice negotiates with foremen or rate-fixers concerning the adjustment of particular piece-work prices. In practice the tendency has, for many years, been in the direction of such bargaining, and the war has very greatly accelerated this tendency. The shop stewards in well-organised workshops have been called upon to play an increasingly important part in determining generally what workmen are to perform particular classes of work, and the prices that are to be paid for particular jobs.

A further step is taken when the Works Committee sets before itself the task of getting prices fixed on a more or less scientific or uniform basis, and, not contenting itself with day-to-day bargaining, attempts to make all the bargaining into which it enters conform to definite principles. In such cases, which are at present none too frequent, the Works Committee, or its secretary, will keep a book or books of prices, in which they will enter the prices agreed upon for particular jobs. These prices will then be used as a basis for negotiations with the management concerning future jobs, and in this way a rudimentary price list will be evolved. Such a price list of course is in no way the same as the agreed printed price lists which we examined in a previous chapter ; it may, however, easily form the foundation upon which such written and agreed lists of prices may be based.

The need for some more developed and scientific form of collective bargaining in the workshop, wherever systems of payments by results are in operation, seems to be too clear to need detailed argument. It exists even in those cases in which the price to be paid for every job is formally regulated by an agreed price list extending over a whole district, or even nationally. For even the existence of such lists does not and cannot, as we have seen, altogether eliminate the need for collective workshop bargaining on matters arising out of the detailed adjustment of prices. In the cotton industry, even when the most elaborate lists have been agreed upon between the Trade Unions and the Employers' Associations, such questions as those of bad material and defective machinery still remain for adjustment, and these require the existence of special workshop machinery.

The growth of the shop stewards' movement during the war seemed for a time to hold out an excellent prospect, in the engineering trades at least, of development along these lines. For a few years practically the whole industry was covered with a network of shop organisations. This growth forced both Unions and employers to draw up terms of formal recognition under the national Shop Stewards' Agreements of 1919 and 1920. The unemployment of post-war years, however, changed the case; and, while the recognised shop steward has now gained a permanent place in collective bargaining, the expected results have not followed. They may yet; but the power of workshop bargaining depends essentially on the condition of trade. Men in fear of unemployment dare not beard the employer in his own works.

If the need for workshop machinery is manifest even where detailed price lists exist, it is far more manifest in the absence of such detailed methods of price-fixing. Where, as in engineering, the fixing of prices is inevitably to a large extent a workshop problem, it is clear that the Trade Unions must establish workshop machinery for this purpose if they are to preserve any regular control at all over the prices to be paid. The policy hitherto largely pursued by the Engineering Unions of discouraging piece-work and other systems of payment by results, and at the same time of leaving such systems unregulated where they are introduced, is a suicidal policy. It has proved in practice impossible to check the gradual extension of payment by results, and the result has mainly been that systems of payment by results have been introduced under the worst possible conditions from the Trade Union point of view. There is, therefore, the most urgent need not merely for the development of workshop machinery capable of taking an effective hand in the fixing and adjusting of prices, but also for giving to such workshop machinery the fullest possible recognition in the official constitution of Trade Unionism. The creation of workshop machinery is necessary for its own sake: recognition of it by the Trade Unions is necessary in order that Workshop Committees may be prevented from making bargains which are inimical to the best interests of Trade Unions, and may be strengthened in their bargaining by the collective backing of the Labour movement.

We have, then, to consider in what way the machinery of collective bargaining in the workshop can be established and extended. In the first place, it would seem clear that shop stewards and Works Committees should be the official representatives of their Trade Unions, or of Federations of Trade Unions where such exist. The practice with regard to official recognition of shop stewards at present varies widely from district to district. Many of the war-time shop stewards were wholly unofficial, that is to say, they were elected by the men in the shop without reference to, or ratification by, any Trade Union organisation. Such unofficial stewards may represent the workmen in the establishment belonging to a particular Trade Union or the workmen of a particular craft irrespective of the Union to which they belong; but in either case they have no constitutional relationship with the Trade Union machinery outside the workshop. Other stewards—and this is true of practically all pre-war stewards, and is still true of the majority—are elected by the men in the workshop, but ratified by the Branch or District Committee of the Union to which they belong. Even in such cases the steward may, in addition to his official functions, exercise many unofficial functions which are not recognised by his Union.

So far we have been dealing only with the recognition of individual stewards by Trade Unions. The stewards, however, in a works usually tend to come together in a Works Committee, or in large works, in a number of Workshop Committees for the different departments, often co-ordinated in a central Works Committee. Most Trade Unions, in the engineering industry at all events, at present make no provision for the recognition of such Works Committees, although in practice many Works Committees are semi-officially or unofficially recognised.

The first case known to the present writer in which a comprehensive system of Trade Union recognition arose was that of Coventry, where the various Engineering unions are federated in a Joint Committee including all the principal Societies. In this scheme no shop steward holds his card from any particular Trade Union; all stewards hold their cards from the Joint Committee. Moreover, provision is made under rules formulated by the Joint Committee for Works Committees and Workshop Committees. All the stewards in a particular workshop elect a chief steward, and the chief stewards from the various shops form the Works Committee. Grievances that cannot be dealt with in the shop are referred to the Works Committee, and the Works Committee refers, where necessary, to the Joint Committee representing the whole district. Matters of principle must always be referred to the Joint Committee.[1]

It would seem that the system adopted in Coventry is capable, with or without modifications, of something like general adoption, and that it would represent a big step forward in the direction of recognition. The Coventry Committee is especially to be commended for the fact that it includes representatives, not only of skilled workers, but also of less skilled. This, however, is comparatively rare, and in most districts the shop stewards' organisations consist wholly of the representatives of the skilled workers, the less skilled Unions and the women being either unrepresented or having separate stewards of their own who are not included on the Committees. The present state of disunity amongst the Trade

[1] This paragraph applies to the war period especially.

Unions in the engineering industry, both among the skilled Unions themselves and as between the Unions representing skilled and less skilled workers, militates very strongly against the adoption of the Coventry system in many centres. It is, however, obviously desirable that this system, or the nearest approach to it that is practicable, should be generally adopted.

Having said this much on the subject of the machinery to be set up, we can now turn to the functions which this machinery might discharge in relation to questions of wage-payment. Obviously if collective bargaining in the workshop is to take place on equal terms between the management and the workers, the first thing the workers require is knowledge equal to that of the employers. Although there still survive many works in which the fixing of prices is purely a haphazard matter, the number of such works is rapidly on the decrease. In most works there are now more or less elaborate departments devoted to the fixing and adjusting of prices, and these departments have in their possession accumulated data which enable them to fix prices on a more or less "scientific" basis. Clearly, the workmen need a corresponding organisation. The price book kept by some Works Committees is a first step in this direction, since to some extent it does supply the workers with data on which to base their bargaining. But the price book by itself is not adequate, especially in those shops which proceed in the fixing of prices by the scientific methods which we have examined in previous chapters. If the employer adopts the method of time-study, the workmen must have some means of countering the data which the employer thus accumulates, or else the bargains arrived at will inevitably be one-sided, or at least dependent on the good-will of the employer.

Suggestions have often been made as to possible methods of meeting this difficulty. Mr. Sidney Webb, in his book, *The Works Manager To-day*, urges very strongly the need for the adoption by the Trade Unions of the method already practised by many employers. The employer in the "scientific" works, at any rate, keeps a salaried rate-fixer, or staff of rate-fixers, whose work it is to see that piece-work prices are on what the management regards as a fair scale. Mr. Webb suggests that what the Trade Unions require is rate-fixers of their own, equally well trained, and able to bargain with the employer's rate-fixers on equal terms.

It is obviously impossible in the present state of Trade Union organisation to hope that the Trade Unions can adopt this suggestion in any complete form. The idea of a salaried Trade Union official employed for full time as an expert rate-fixer in every works is at any rate not immediately realisable, if only on account of the cost which it would entail. Mr. Webb very rightly points out that the miners have already in each pit an official who corresponds to some extent to the salaried rate-fixer suggested. The checkweighman in the colliery is an official appointed by the men and paid by them, whose business it is to see that they are not defrauded in tonnage payments, and otherwise to look after their interests inside the colliery. There is obviously no final reason why a similar method should not be employed in every large works or factory throughout the country, although it is doubtful whether one official for each works would be anything like enough, since in any complicated factory many different processes are carried out, and these processes are sometimes so divergent in character as to require different kinds of skill for the fixing of rates. The employer may have several rate-fixers or time-study men in his works, and there seems no final reason why the Trade Unions should be content with less.

It is, however, only by looking well ahead that we can envisage any such development. We may hope that it will come, and believe that it is bound to come as the Trade Unions develop a policy directed to securing greater control over industry; but for the immediate future it is possible to make a suggestion that is capable of being put at once into effect. At present the Trade Unions as national bodies have, for the most part, no expert staff for dealing with problems of wage-payment; they have their executives, secretaries, and organisers, but these officials have to deal with every kind of Trade Union problem, and have no time or opportunity to specialise on methods of wage-payment. It is true that this cannot be said of all Trade Unions in equal measure. For instance, the officials of the Cotton Trade Unions are largely, if not primarily, experts in wage-payment, and it has often been argued that their general organising and propagandist work suffers as the effect of their specialisation upon problems of wage-payment. Moreover, as we saw in an earlier chapter, the Boilermakers and certain other Trade Unions do employ experts whose main business it is to negotiate on such questions; but the supply of Trade Union experts in wage-payment runs out just where the need is greatest—in the Unions in which no organised methods of determining prices exist. If there is need among the Cotton Unions and among the Boilermakers for experts of this class, there is infinitely more need for them in the engineering industry. Why, then, cannot the Engineering Trade Unions make a beginning by establishing a limited number of permanent officials who are experts on these questions, and give to these permanent officials the function of offering advice to local and works bodies wherever such advice is needed, of visiting the particular works or districts for purposes of negotiation wherever it is proposed to introduce new systems, and of going into a shop or district to settle disputes arising out of the adjustment of prices wherever such disputes have arisen? The establishment even of a small number of such officials, equipped with special training equal to that of the experts retained by the employers, would enormously increase the bargaining power of the Trade Unions. At present the Trade Unions in the engineering industry, and in many other industries, are efficient in bargaining so far as the general level of wages in a district is concerned. But, even when general wage levels have been determined, there still remain very large possibilities for leakage of earnings in consequence of defective fixing of prices, and it is certain that the adoption of more scientific methods by the Trade Unions in dealing with such questions would add very largely to the gross earnings of their members.

The evolution of industry is undoubtedly in the direction of a more scientific adjustment of payment for work done from the employer's point of view. The employers are developing with great rapidity more exact systems of determining and adjusting piece-work prices, and are increasing their staff of salaried experts devoted to this purpose alone. Such action on the one side surely calls for action on the other, and it is difficult to see how the Trade Unions can much longer resist so urgent a demand, unless, indeed, they are prepared not merely to demand, but also to enforce, the abolition of all systems of payment by results. This seems, to say the least of it, an improbable contingency at the present stage.

It is not suggested that a few salaried officials could settle the problem from the Trade Union point of view. Indeed, they would only form the basis upon which a more comprehensive system could be built up. There is need, as we have seen, for machinery in each particular works and workshop, and here, if the final remedy lies largely in the selection of salaried experts in each works, a more immediate solution lies in the development of the Works Committee. We mentioned in an early part of this book [1] the scheme, put forward under the auspices of the Paisley Trades Council by two prominent Engineering Trade Unionists, under which the workers in each shop, instead of driving individual piece-work bargains with their employers, would contract collectively for the whole output of the shop, agreeing by collective bargaining upon the price to be paid for the work done. For the assumption of such functions, however desirable it may be, the Trade Unions are not at present equipped. They need first a much greater extension of workshop machinery and a selection of their workshop representatives more with a view to effective workshop bargaining on such matters. It should be regarded as necessary for the Workshop Committee, in addition to its ordinary members dealing with general workshop problems, to have on it at least one man whose special business it is to look after piece-work prices, standard times, etc., and to equip himself with the special knowledge that is necessary in order to make collective bargaining effective. Such a specialised shop steward could have charge of the shop price book ; he could be recognised by his Trade Union ; and he could receive part-time payment for services rendered in the same way as every local part-time Trade Union official.

I do not know whether the foregoing suggestions will seem too modest or too Utopian ; but I am sure of this, that, if Trade

[1] See p. 36.

Unionists in the workshops really mean what they are saying about getting greater control over industry, they will be forced inevitably in the direction which I have indicated. The employer needs for his control over industry a huge staff of salaried experts, and this staff is continually increasing in numbers. If the Trade Unions are to control industry they will need their salaried staff just as much as the employers. It is of no use to put forward the demand for control without being prepared to provide the means by which alone control, even in the limited sphere of the workshop, can be made effective.

CHAPTER XII

COMMISSION SYSTEMS

AKIN to the systems of payment by results which we have described in this book are the various systems, prevailing especially in the distributive trades, by which a commission on sales is given to various classes of workers. A frequent practice in large retail houses is to provide for the payment to their branch managers, and sometimes to the whole staff in their shops, of a time-rate of wages *plus* a commission in some way dependent on the turnover or profits of the branch. Sometimes this commission is based simply on turnover, sometimes it is a sort of output bonus on sales over a given standard minimum, sometimes it is based not on sales but on profits, and sometimes, as in the case of the model rules issued some years ago by the Co-operative Union to Co-operative Distributive Stores, on a curious blending of total sales with profits realised.[1]

Also, it should be noted that such commissions may be paid on either an individual or a collective basis. Each individual may be paid a bonus or commission on his individual turnover, or the whole of the employees in the shop or store may be paid a commission at varying rates on the gross turnover of the shop.

This system is by no means confined to the retail distributive trades. It is almost universally in vogue in the case of commercial travellers, agents, and canvassers in the wholesale trades, and applies not only to canvassers for the sales of goods, but also to such other canvassers for orders as insurance agents. The bonus or commission may represent a larger or smaller proportion of the total earnings. In some cases a relatively high time salary is secured, and a relatively small bonus is paid on top of this. In others, however, the time-rate of wages or salary allowed is exceedingly small, and the employee is mainly dependent for his earnings on the amount of commission which he can secure. Obviously where this is the case the position of the employee is exceedingly precarious, and the door is open to all kinds of abuses. The insurance agents have long protested in vain against the unfair systems

[1] See Schloss, *Methods of Industrial Remuneration*, p. 327.

of commission earnings on which they are paid, and both among shop assistants in private employment and among co-operative employees there have been repeated efforts to destroy the system altogether. It is, however, sometimes popular with persons earning a relatively high rate of salary, especially with managers of various sorts, and sometimes, while the assistants are anxious for its abolition, the manager desires to retain it. In the distributive trades there is no doubt that it is very widely extended to the managers of branch shops of all kinds.

Indeed, there is ample evidence that very similar systems extend a very long way up the ladder of industry. Managers of great productive works in many cases receive, in addition to their salary, either a sort of bonus on output, or at least a share in profits. The managing director, working under such a system, no doubt does not usually think of it as in essence the same as the system which he is trying to impose upon his employees under the name of payment by results, but there is no doubt as to their essential similarity.

The Trade Union movement has naturally for the most part set its face against the commission system in all its forms, and wherever Trade Unionism has become strong, if the system has not been altogether destroyed, at any rate its abuses have been very greatly mitigated. Thus, just as among manual workers payment by results is only tolerated, if at all, where a standard day-wage is guaranteed, so workers under commission systems always endeavour to secure an upstanding salary on a fair basis, and are only willing, if at all, to agree to commission systems when such a salary has been secured.

We have seen that systems of payment by results encounter far less opposition in trades in which output can readily be measured in terms of effort than in those in which there is a wide variation in the results secured by the same effort on different occasions. Obviously if this is a fair criterion, the trades to which commission systems are principally applied are among the least suited for payment by results in any form. The earnings of an insurance agent are not mainly dependent upon the effort which he puts forward, and the same effort on different occasions will produce very different results. Earnings in such cases are very largely dependent on the personality of the worker; one man will wheedle premiums out of a reluctant housewife where another man who puts forth at least the same effort will repeatedly fail. This in some measure distinguishes commission systems from other forms of payment by results. They are largely a payment for personality, if not always for the most desirable type of personality, whereas the systems of payment by results which apply to productive industry are based mainly on the ignoring of personality, good or bad, and have an eye solely or mainly to mechanical efficiency at a particular job.

Similar in some respects to commission systems are "tip" systems. Waiters and other attendants, porters at railway stations, and certain other classes of workers are often paid relatively small time-rates of wages, or sometimes no wages at all, in the expectation that their earnings will be made up by "tips." Sometimes the wages paid are even a minus quantity, and persons pay to be employed for the sake of the tips which they can secure. The social objections to this system are obvious, and repeated attempts have been made to secure its abolition, or at least to bring it under social control. These attempts have been largely unsuccessful, although under the patronage of Messrs. Lyons the "no tip" restaurant and the "no tip" hotel had made a certain amount of headway before the war, while the action of the National Union of Railwaymen on the railways had been directed to securing for the porter at least a guaranteed living wage independent of "tips." Nevertheless, there still remains a considerable proportion of the population on the verge of industry which subsists largely on highly variable "tips" given by the public, ranging from the almost standardised "tip" of the Oxford college "scout," or Cambridge "gyp," to the extremely variable earnings of railway guards for winking at disregard of the Company's regulations, or for looking after juvenile or decrepit travellers.

Probably, until Great Britain becomes a democracy in fact, as well as in name, this unpleasant system of payment, not for work done, but for getting on the right side of people, will continue. No attempt has been made to deal with this problem here on a scientific basis, because it is itself fundamentally unscientific and variable, and insusceptible of detailed examination.

CHAPTER XIII

PROFIT-SHARING AS A FORM OF PAYMENT BY RESULTS

It is not proposed in this chapter to attempt any general examination of profit-sharing or of the social motives and results behind it. That would take us too far away from our main subject. But it is necessary to say something of profit-sharing in relation to our subject because it is sometimes suggested that profit-sharing may offer an alternative to payment by results. The usual reason adduced for the introduction of systems of payment by results is that a stimulus to effort on the part of the individual worker is needed. It has sometimes been held by employers that this stimulus can be secured by giving to the employee a share in the profits instead of paying him in correspondence with his daily or weekly output. For example, a large engineering firm, during the war, put forward a scheme under which complete abolition of payment by results was suggested, and at the same time proposed to institute a general scheme of profit-sharing.

It is more than doubtful whether profit-sharing, where it has been adopted, has secured the results desired by those who have introduced it. The period over which a share in profits is spread is necessarily a long one, and the workmen, as a rule, do not look very far ahead. Normally a worker is hardly likely to be stimulated to greater effort by the knowledge that, if he and his fellows work exceptionally hard to-day, they may in some degree share in the profits of the firm a year hence, and thereby secure some addition to their earnings. This is, of course, a purely utilitarian argument directed to show that profit-sharing in most cases will not in effect secure the results expected from it by employers.

There is, however, a far more serious argument against profit-sharing in all its forms. The case put forward for systems of payment by results is that output is to a large extent within the worker's own control; that he can, by additional effort, secure additional results. This is only true to a limited extent even of output; but it is far less true of profits. The profits of a firm depend partly, no doubt, upon the skill and intelligence of the workers whom it employs; but they depend to a considerably greater extent in many trades upon the general industrial situation, the state of the market, and so on, and upon the factor of good or bad management. Bad management or a bad sales department may sweep away all the extra efficiency which has resulted from an increase of effort on the part of the workers, and this argument, which is fatal to the theoretical basis of profit-sharing, has been used with devastating effect by Sir W. J. Ashley.[1] If it is fatal to profit-sharing as a system, it is certainly no less fatal to profit-sharing regarded as an alternative to payment by results.

The case put forward by the advocates of profit-sharing is usually that the workman's skill and strength are equivalent to the money capital of the shareholder, or the business ability of the manager, and that all alike are entitled to their dividend on the " capital " which they put into the business. This, of course, is an argument based upon the assumption that capitalist standards of value are correct, that the capitalist as an owner of money or productive plant is entitled to a dividend. It is, in fact, merely an extension of capitalist morality to include the working class. Those who hold that capital is not entitled to any dividend at all are hardly likely to look favourably upon a proposal to " capitalise " the human energy of the worker.

It is true that, under the existing system, it is not easy for the workers to escape altogether from profit-sharing in one form or another. Even where there is no overt system of sharing profits, an increase in the prosperity of a trade normally brings with it an increase in wages, although this is often balanced by a corresponding rise in prices. Such increases (or corresponding decreases in times of bad trade) of course apply not to the prosperity of particular works, but to that of whole trades. They are therefore in one sense fundamentally different in character from profit-sharing schemes; but there is a fundamental similarity which deserves attention. More particularly in those industries in which wages are assessed on a sliding-scale system is there a close approach to the system of profit-sharing. In many branches of the iron and steel industry, for instance, wage fluctuations are dependent upon the selling price of the product under sliding scales with or without maxima and minima. Now, an increase in the selling price is not necessarily accompanied by an increase in profits, but it usually tends to be so accompanied, and in effect, when the workers' wages go up, it generally means that the employer's dividends have gone up too. A similar system in somewhat less rigid form, but presenting essentially the same features, exists over a good part of the coal industry, where wage fluctuations are in practice mainly determined by changes in the price of coal. Moreover, even where there is no ostensible agreement to base wages solely or partly upon selling prices it is almost inevitable that the prosperity of a trade should be taken into account when wages claims are under consideration.

[1] *Quarterly Review*, October 1913.

To this extent workers under the wage system are almost inevitably profit-sharers; but an entirely new principle is introduced when it is proposed to use profit-sharing as a definite inducement to higher production. It is not denied that this inducement may, in particular cases, be effective, particularly in the case of old employees or of firms which have something of a "family" character about them; but it is quite clear that the system is not capable of general extension, or, at any rate, if generally extended, would not produce the expected results. How far profit-sharing schemes have been in the past instrumental in providing any real stimulus to output can be judged from the fact that on the average they have meant an addition of 5 per cent or 6 per cent to wages. What self-respecting workman would work piece-work for earnings of 6 per cent over his time-rate? The answer is, of course, that in the organised trades the piece-worker, normally, expects earnings on a considerably higher level, and that he is only prepared to work piece-work at all on the understanding that he will earn at least, on the average, time and a third, that is to say, 33⅓ per cent as a minimum, as against the 5 per cent average of the profit-sharers. Even 33⅓ per cent does not represent, by any means, what the piece-worker is now inclined to expect, or what he will be inclined to accept under favourable trade conditions.

Nothing has been said in this chapter of the adverse effects of profit-sharing upon Trade Unions; indeed, we can hardly deal with that matter here effectively, because the effects of profit-sharing are to a great extent the effects of payment by results in an intensified form. There can be no doubt that the adoption of profit-sharing by a particular firm does tend to divide the workers in that firm from workers in other employment, and to some extent to substitute for their loyalty to the working class loyalty to a particular employer. It breaks up the solidarity of Labour, and substitutes a host of competing solidarities attached to particular firms. The dream has sometimes been dreamt of universal systems of profit-sharing applying, not to any particular firm, but over whole industries, and even not to particular workers, but to associations of workers. That is to say, schemes of profit-sharing have been suggested, not between employers and their employees, but between Employers' Associations and Trade Unions. The anti-social tendencies of any such schemes from the point of view of the community seem too obvious to require comment, but perhaps in these days of Whitley Councils it is just necessary to draw attention to them. It is at any rate clear that profit-sharing on such a universal basis would have no connection with payment by results, since the incentive to higher production could hardly be spread over an area wider than that of a particular firm.

CHAPTER XIV

PAYMENT BY RESULTS *VERSUS* TIME-WORK

WE have now completed our survey of the various systems of payment by results under the wage system, and it is time to endeavour to form some estimate of their social effects. We have seen that the reception accorded to these systems varies widely from trade to trade. In trades in which the unit of output is highly standardised, so that output is as a rule commensurate with effort, systems of payment by results are for the most part accepted without serious question. In other trades in which either there is no ready unit of measurement, or at least output varies widely from time to time and from case to case, owing to causes which cannot easily be reduced to mathematical formulae, the Trade Unions, wherever they are strong enough, usually offer strong opposition to the adoption of payment by results instead of time-work.

As we saw in an earlier chapter, it is a great mistake to suppose that Trade Unionists are united in favour either of piece-work or of time-work. In the cotton and other textile industries, the piece-work system is hardly questioned. In the mining industry attacks on piece-work are beginning, but have not yet reached any great proportions; in some branches of shipbuilding piece-work is extremely popular among the workers, in others time-work is rigidly adhered to. In some cases the skilled workmen insist upon piece-work conditions, and at the same time acquiesce in, or even insist on, the exclusion of their unskilled assistants from any share in the results. In such cases the unskilled workers are found most strongly demanding their inclusion in the piece-work systems applying to "squad" or "gang" work of various sorts.

On the whole, unskilled workers in organised trades tend to be more favourable to payment by results than skilled workers. The skilled worker is assured of a fairly high level of earnings, even under time-work conditions, while the unskilled worker has every inducement to endeavour to supplement his extremely low time-work rate of wages by piece-work earnings. It may be held that the remedy lies in the raising of the time-work rate; but in practice in the past the time-work rates of the unskilled workers have been largely determined by those of the skilled workers. As the skilled workman has usually not shown himself as sympathetic as he might be towards the unskilled, it is no wonder that the unskilled are driven to ask for payment by results as a means of supplementing their earnings.

We are, however, concerned here not so much with the present attitude of various types and classes of workers to payment by results, as with the social desirability of the system in itself. Does payment by results actually conduce to industrial efficiency, and does it tend to produce good citizens?

The question whether payment by results ministers to industrial efficiency is not an easy question to answer in the abstract. It can hardly be doubted that the immediate effect of the adoption of a system of payment by results, where a time-work system has previously been in operation, is usually an increase in output. This means fuller utilisation of machinery, and, from the employer's point of view, greater industrial efficiency. But it is by no means clear that this increase in efficiency is usually maintained. When a system of payment by results has been for a time in operation time-work intensity is often gradually reintroduced, and it is probable that the outstanding instances of "ca' canny" occur rather under systems of payment by results than under time-work. The inducement to slow down artificially exists to the greatest extent where such slowing down may result in an improved piece-work price, or is forced upon the workers as a protection against rate-cutting. It does not exist to the same extent under time-work conditions.

Moreover, it is often argued by the workmen themselves that payment by results is destructive of craftsmanship, and tends to the production of shoddy work. The workman who is paid by the piece, or on some system of output bonus, has every inducement to secure the maximum production, and not to bother about the finish of his work, except in so far as this is necessary in order that it may pass inspection. It can hardly be doubted that, in operations which are not of a purely repetitive and machine-minding character, payment by results has a tendency to produce defective workmanship. The employer, from the point of view of profit, does not mind this unless and until it affects the selling properties of the goods produced. British industry in the past, it is true, has specialised largely on the production of commodities of high quality; but there is a marked tendency at the present time towards "mass production," and insistence upon quantity rather than upon quality. This tendency may be to some extent inevitable, and standardisation may be in certain limited directions a good thing; but from the social, as opposed to the business, point of view, it is not enough to prove that payment by results effects an increase in output or in profits; against such increase has to be set any falling off in the quality of the goods produced under the system, and not only this, but also the falling off in the standard of craftsmanship on the part of the worker.

We have partially answered our second question already. Does payment by results tend to produce good citizens? In so far as it lowers the standard of craftsmanship it clearly does not. It is sometimes urged—by a recent writer, in *Engineering*, for instance—that the social disadvantages of loss of craftsmanship are more than offset by the reduction of hours which mass production makes possible. It is, however, permissible to doubt whether increase of leisure, however necessary and desirable it is, will by itself make better citizens unless the conditions under which work is carried on are themselves such as to create men capable of using their leisure in the right way. It is not at all certain that, from the social point of view, six hours of mass production possess any particular advantages over eight hours of craftsmanship. This is not said with any desire to minimise the importance of reducing hours; it is only suggested that six hours of craftsmanship would be better than either.

Moreover, most of the systems of payment by results which we have analysed connote probably, if not necessarily, a decrease in the control exercised by the workers over the conditions under which their work is carried on, the concentration of industrial power to an increasing extent in the hands of experts retained by the management, and the rendering more difficult of any approach towards industrial self-government by the rank and file of the workers. In our chapter on workshop bargaining we suggested methods by which this tendency might be modified and offset to some extent; but it is almost necessarily present in any systems of payment by results that are likely to be acceptable to employers at the present time. Indeed, the only system of payment by results which is not open to this objection is the system of collective contract, already twice mentioned, which has been put forward by Messrs. Gallagher and Paton in their Memorandum published by the Paisley Trades Council.

The system of collective contract by the whole workshop for all jobs, which would leave the arrangement of work in the shop and the detailed execution of the jobs in the hands of the workers collectively, would represent an increase in industrial democracy, and at the same time would be a method of payment by results on an improved collective basis.

The feeling of the present writer is very strongly in favour of the view that, wherever possible, payment by results should be accepted only on the widest possible collective basis. The systems of output bonus by which a whole shop is paid a bonus on the production of the whole shop are infinitely preferable to any of the systems of individual payment by results. Individual payment by results, however it is safeguarded, inevitably tends to the weakening of the collective bargaining power of the workers, and to the setting of one man's hand against another's. This is true in some degree even of the cotton industry, or in industries in which closely regulated systems of payment by results exist. It is true far more where the element of individual bargaining enters largely, as in engineering and other skilled crafts. A collective system, at any rate, does recognise the group as a unit, and does establish a common solidarity among the workers belonging to the group.

It is sometimes urged against this suggestion that under a collective system of payment by results the workers will tend to speed one another up; but against this must be set the employers' argument that collective systems are no use, because the workers will tend to speed one another down. The moral seems to be that a collective system will result in something like a fair day's work, neither in overstrain nor in "ca' canny," at least where the collective system is accompanied by democratic control in the workshop.

By a collective system is here meant not simply a pool among a number of skilled workmen, but collective payment to a whole workshop, even where the workers in it are engaged on different parts of jobs or on different jobs. So far output bonus systems have, as a rule, only been applied where the output of a shop has been of a uniform and standardised character; but there is no reason why on the lines suggested by the Paisley Memorandum the Workshop Committee should not bargain collectively with the employer for the prices to be paid for each article produced in a shop, however variable the range of products may be. The employer would then pay to the shop a price for each article produced; but the total earnings of the shop would be divided under a shop fellowship system among the whole body of workers, skilled and unskilled.

Such a system would not, of course, end the wage system—it would be simply another form of wage-payment. Piece-work, bonus systems, collective contract, and time-work are all alike merely forms of payment under the wage system, and, as we saw in our first chapter, all these forms of payment have a common basis. The time-worker is inevitably paid a time-rate which has some relation to the output which he is expected to produce, while the piece-worker is paid a piece-work rate which is calculated so as to produce earnings ranging round about an estimated time standard. An output bonus system, or a collective contract system, would necessarily be based on similar principles, and the same applies in effect to suggestions for profit-sharing. There is no way out of the wage system merely by juggling with the method of wage-payment.

We have, then, simply to choose between a number of varied methods of payment under the wage system, and we cannot pronounce unhesitatingly in favour of any of them as of universal applicability. We may, however, try to frame certain generalised conclusions as to the system which is best under a number of very general conditions:

(1) Where the product is standardised, and a given effort will

normally produce a given output, it does not make very much difference from the Trade Union point of view whether the workers are paid by time or by piece. This statement is subject to a reservation to which we shall come shortly.

(2) Where the product is not standardised, and a given effort cannot be relied upon to produce a given output, time-work is the system to be preferred, at all events unless a system of payment by results can be secured which satisfies the two following conditions: (*a*) that it should be a collective system, extending to a large enough group of workers to equalise variations as between one job and another, and one worker and another; and (*b*) that it should include such a measure of democratic workshop control as will secure for the workers a real instalment of industrial self-government.

On these principles it might be said that in the cotton industry there is no considerable argument against payment by results. The mining industry, on account of the abnormal place difficulty, stands on the border-line, and would do well to look towards a collective system of payment extending to all the workers on a particular seam, while the engineering industry, except on repetition work, could only be expected reasonably to accept payment by results on a broad collective basis, and combined with workshop control.

It is always necessary in this connection to draw attention to the fact that, when collective payment by results is spoken of, the reference is to systems in which all workers share in the pool. The "butty" system in the mines, on the other hand, and the "piece-master" system in some metal and wood-working trades, are among the worst abuses of the wage system. Under them the top dog takes more than his fair share of the earnings, and virtually employs the bottom dog at a wholly inadequate time-rate. No pooling system is really equitable from the Trade Union point of view unless all the workers concerned share fully in the pool.

So much for the immediate question; but we cannot leave the subject without looking rather further into the future. It is often suggested that payment by results possesses some superior equity over time-work, in that it does secure that a worker who produces more will get more money. This, in the mind of the present writer, is pure capitalist morality. Why should a man who produces more be paid more? It is true that workmen have sometimes argued that what they want is a larger share in the wealth they produce, and the elimination of the surplus value at present pocketed by the capitalist has been confused with the appropriation of this value by each individual productive worker or group of workers. But surely what we are out for is not that each man should secure in full the fruit of his own labour, but that the fruits of the common labour of all should be equitably shared among all. The idea of paying men for work done may have a certain element of superiority over the present system under which men are paid principally for work which they do not do, and are paid less in proportion as their work is unpleasant or heavy ; but payment for work done is surely not the last word in industrial morality. Bernard Shaw's argument for equality of income seems to the present writer to be convincing when it is clearly understood. It is often misunderstood and misdescribed as a plea for equality of "remuneration," whereas Bernard Shaw's whole point is that the idea of remuneration is in itself wrong, that people ought not to be remunerated for the work which they do, but ought to be assured of an income by virtue of their citizenship, or by virtue of the fact that they are human beings. Equality of income (not remuneration) is not indeed an ideal ; but it is the nearest working approximation to an ideal sharing of the wealth of the community. Time-work has at least this advantage over payment by results—that it does normally secure equality of remuneration to all the workers who are doing the same kind of job. It does not make much approach to equality of income or even to equality of remuneration as between workers doing different types of work ; but it is almost universally recognised that time-work does in a certain sense convey a higher status than payment by results, and this is more especially the case where, instead of a wage which lapses in the case of sickness, and does not afford any security of employment, the worker is paid an upstanding salary, irrespective of the actual hours put in on his job. The civil servant is in a sense a time-worker, or at any rate is more like a time-worker than a piece-worker, and the civil servant certainly acquires by the fact that he is not paid by results a superior status to the piece-worker whose earnings are dependent on his actual output. Piece-work and other systems of payment by results, even if they result in an increase of earnings, do seem to the present writer to result in a loss of status, and to those who regard status as of greater ultimate importance to the working class than immediate earnings under the wage system, the arguments in favour of time-work on purely social grounds appear to be convincing. Indeed, were the system of collective contract outlined in the Paisley Memorandum to be accepted, it would surely be better for the workers included in the contract to pay collectively to each of their number an upstanding salary, and to use the balance, not for division, but for other purposes, such as the building up of their Trade Union organisation, or the provision of special benefits or amenities, or the reduction of hours spent on the work. The upstanding salary is still subject in large measure to the conditions of the wage system ; but it is the first upward step out of that system, and, if for this reason alone, the securing of it should be the immediate object of the working class.

CHAPTER XV

THE PROBLEM FOR TRADE UNIONISTS

THE last chapter represents in substance an appeal to idealism, but it is necessary to consider for a moment what the working classes ought to do in regard to payment by results, if they either do not feel sufficiently idealistic to take the course recommended in the last chapters or are not strong enough to enforce their demands in that direction. It is no use to deny the fact that in many centres of industry in which individual systems of payment by results are established, the workers would at present oppose their abolition. As I have indicated, in my view the right method to adopt wherever possible in such cases is to endeavour to convert individual into collective systems; but even this may be in some cases impossible, or exceedingly difficult of attainment. It cannot be too strongly urged that wherever a system of payment by results, whether individual or collective, is in operation, the workers must secure over that system a collective control. Such control can only be secured if the working classes have in their possession as complete and scientific a method as the employers. I have indicated in an earlier chapter possible lines upon which Trade Unions might develop scientific methods in bargaining about piece-work prices, and in this concluding chapter all that I desire to do is to stress once more the paramount necessity for dealing immediately with this question. It is a suicidal policy for the Trade Unions to leave payment by results unregulated, or to attempt to confront the scientific experts or the employers without equally scientific knowledge in their own hands. If payment by results is to go on, and, still more, if the workers are to secure any real control over industry, they must concentrate on getting, in their own ranks, men with a real understanding of workshop problems, including especially problems of wage-payment.

This is not, in effect, a particularly difficult task. There are thousands of men in the Trade Union Movement who could quite easily be fitted for the work in question, if the proper training were provided. It is only the fact that the Trade Union Movement has not hitherto, except in isolated instances, realised the need for such training, or been prepared to pay for it, that has held the Trade Unions back from securing the right men or the amount of "science in industry" to equal the development on the employers' side. The Trade Unions must either develop a science of their own or else they must relinquish any claim to a real control over industrial conditions. If they prefer to relinquish their claim, they may secure higher wages, and even shorter hours and better conditions in the workshop, but they will not secure self-government or democracy, either in industry or elsewhere; for the conditions which prevail in the workshop inevitably condition and govern the conditions which prevail in men's social relationships. If the industrial system is one which divorces the worker from control, and places him in the hands of the expert as a mere machine-minder, not even the most ample leisure will suffice to make him a good citizen. The conditions of his work will not develop in him any initiative or capacity for self-government, and it is only by these qualities that he can hope to overthrow the existing system in industry and politics, and to replace it by a system of democracy.

The Trade Unions, then, have a clear choice before them, and their choice, even in what seems so restricted a sphere as that of wage-payment, may well play an important part in determining, not merely the industrial future, but also the future constitution of the social system.

APPENDIX A

PIECE-WORK PROVISIONS OF ENGINEERING AGREEMENTS

THE following are the provisions (see next page) regarding piece-work in the three engineering agreements of 1897 (following the great engineering lock-out), 1901, and 1907. The 1907 agreement was terminated in 1914 by the Amalgamated Society of Engineers. It will be noted that the three agreements showed a progressive evolution of safeguards for piece-work, and that further improvements were secured in the special Piece-work Agreement of 1919.

PIECE-WORK AGREEMENT, 1919

Where, by reason of the introduction of the 47-hour week,[1] a workman is not able to earn on piece-work his previous remuneration on the same job, the employers will undertake to recommend that suitable adjustments shall be made on the piece-work price for that job.

It is agreed that piece-work prices should be such as will enable a workman of average ability to earn at least 33⅓ per cent over present time rates (excluding war bonuses). Piece-work prices once established shall not be altered unless the means or method of manufacture is changed.

Meantime, it is agreed that when prices are such that on account of the reduction in hours the workman of average ability is unable to earn 33⅓ per cent, the necessary adjustment should be made.

[1] Introduced in 1919.

[TABLE

ENGINEERING AGREEMENTS

Provisions regarding Piece-work

1907.	1901.	1897.
Employers and their workmen are entitled to work piece-work, provided : (*a*) The prices to be paid shall be fixed by mutual arrangement between the employer and the workman or workmen who perform the work. (*b*) Each workman's day-rate to be guaranteed irrespectively of his piece-work earnings. (*c*) Overtime and nightshift to be paid in addition to piece-work prices, on the same conditions as already prevail in each workshop for time-work.	Employers and their workmen have the right to work piece-work. The prices to be paid for piece-work shall be fixed by mutual arrangement between the employer and the workman or workmen who perform the work, and the employers guarantee that they shall be such as will allow a workman of average efficiency to earn at least his time-rate of wages, with increased earnings for increased production due to additional exertion on his part.	The right to work piece-work at present exercised by many of the Federated Employers shall be extended to all members of the Federation and to all their Union workmen. The prices to be paid for piece-work shall be fixed by mutual arrangement between the employer and the workman or workmen who perform the work.
	The Federation will discountenance any arrangement or rearrangement of prices which will not allow a workman to obtain increased earnings in respect of increased production due to such additional exertion, and the Trade Unions will discountenance any restriction of output.	The Federation will not countenance any piece-work conditions which will not allow a workman of average efficiency to earn at least the wage at which he is rated.
All balances and wages to be paid through the office.	The Federation agree to recommend that all wages and balances should be paid through the office.	The Federation recommend that all wages and balances shall be paid through the office. *Note.*—These are just the conditions that have been for long in force in various shops. Individual workmen are much benefited by piece-work.
	A mutual arrangement as to piece-work rates between employer and workman in no way interferes with the Trade Unions arranging with their own members the rates and conditions under which they shall work.	A mutual arrangement as to piece-work rates between employer and workman in no way interferes with the functions of the Unions in arranging with their own members the rates and conditions under which they shall work.

APPENDIX B

PIECE-WORK RULES OF TRADE UNIONS IN THE ENGINEERING, SHIPBUILDING, AND SMALLER METAL TRADES

THE following extracts from the Rule Books of selected Trade Unions in the engineering and kindred industries illustrate very clearly the lack of systematic regulation or of uniform systems. At the same time, they serve to bring out the fact that a good deal of rudimentary collective bargaining exists, and that, in some of the smaller metal trades especially, the method of the piece-work list has been adopted in a more or less developed form. It will be seen that, in the majority of cases, the Rules are designed to discourage piece-work, and that the impossibility of dispensing with it altogether is often recognised with reluctance. It should also be noted that some of the Rules have developed by a process of gradual amendment out of Rules originally designed to combat sub-contracting.

PIECE-WORK RULES

AMALGAMATED SOCIETY OF ENGINEERS. Rule 39.[1]

1. Any member asking for or taking work by contract or piece-work contrary to conditions here following, in any firm or factory where piece or contract work does not at present exist, and the same being proved to the satisfaction of the District Committee, shall for the first offence be fined 20s., for the second 40s., and for the third be expelled from the Society. Piece-work, however, may be worked subject to conditions here following, and providing that the minimum rate of wages of the district be fully guaranteed by the firm introducing it.

2. All members engaged on piece-work shall, as far as possible, make it imperative that they be paid through the pay office, and not by a piece-master. Where this is not possible they shall, upon the request of their Branch or the District Committee, produce their pay sheet. District Committees shall see that members have a proper rated wage guaranteed, apart altogether from piece prices, and in cases where members are working piece-work, the District Committee shall draw up rules by which it shall be governed, so as to protect our members against the action of employers who seek to interfere with the minimum wages of the district.

3. Any member taking work by the piece or contract, and not sharing equally in proportion to his wages any surplus made over and above the weekly wages paid to members and other persons working on such job, shall be summoned before his Branch or Branch Committee, and if he does not comply with the above regulation he shall be fined in the first instance 20s., second 40s., and in the third instance be excluded, subject to the approval of the Council.

4. Any member found to be using his influence to discharge, or cause to be discharged or suspended, men working on any piece or contract job, who

[1] The corresponding rule of the Amalgamated Engineering Union (1926), into which the A.S E has been absorbed, reads as follows, and may serve as typical of changes in the engineering position since this book was written :

" (*a*) No member shall ask for or take work by any system of payment by results or contract in any firm or factory where such system of payment does not exist without the approval of and in conformity with the conditions as laid down by the District Committee.

" (*b*) Piece-work shall only be accepted on the basis of the district rate of wages being guaranteed, and prices shall be such as will enable a workman of average ability to earn at least 33⅓ per cent over day rates, and where a reduction in the hours of working takes place suitable adjustments shall be made in the piece-work prices. All members engaged on piece-work shall make it imperative that they be paid through the pay office.

" (*c*) [Repeats the provisions of 3 and 5, above.]

" (*d*) [Repeats the provisions of 4, above.] "

are in receipt of the ordinary rates or wages of the district, and substituting boy labour or cheaper labour in their place for the purpose of making surpluses over and above the rate of the day wages of the district, shall be for the first offence fined 40s., for the second 60s., and for the third excluded; such penalties, with the reason thereof, to be posted in a conspicuous place in all the club-rooms of the district; the District Committee secretary to furnish each branch secretary with the necessary information.

5. Any member working for or under any piece-master, and not receiving an equal share of any surplus in proportion that may be made over and above his weekly wages shall be summoned before the Branch, Branch Committee, or District Committee; and, on his refusing to leave such employment he shall be fined for the first offence 20s., for the second offence 40s., and for the third offence excluded, subject to the approval of the Council.

Steam-engine Makers' Society. Rule 46.

This rule is identical in substance with that of the A.S.E.

Amalgamated Toolmakers. Rule 55, Section 1.

1. In no case shall members of this Society work on any job at less price than that paid previously, unless such wage was above the minimum rate of the district for that class of work. Any member unknowingly commencing to work in contravention of the above shall, as soon as he becomes aware of it (unless at once paid the proper price) immediately give notice to leave, and acquaint his committee with the circumstances, upon which he will be entitled to donation as per rule. In case of any member breaking this section his conduct shall be brought before his Branch Committee, and he shall be fined a sum not exceeding £1, or expelled the society.

United Machine Workers' Association. Rule 26.

1. In the event of any of our members being called upon to work piece-work or Premium Bonus System, day-rates must be guaranteed, and any member asking for or introducing piece-work into shops where not already introduced (on the same being proven to the satisfaction of his Branch) shall be fined for the first offence £1, on the second excluded, and all members working in boiler shops and shipyards shall be governed by the conditions existing in those departments.

Electrical Trades Union. Rule 37.

420. Members are not to consider that because the following penalties are attached to members working piece-work, the Union looks upon the system with the slightest degree of favour, but, on the contrary, the Union considers it one of the greatest evils it has to contend with, and it therefore becomes the duty of every member permanently to dispense with piece-work whenever an opportunity presents itself, and certainly to prevent its introduction into any shop or district where it does not exist.

421. Any member asking for or taking work by contract or piece-work in any shop where contract or piece-work does not at present exist, the same being proved to the satisfaction of his Branch or Branch Committee, shall for the first offence be fined 20s., and for the second be excluded, subject to the approval of the Executive Council. All District Committees and Branches are to see that all members have a proper rated wage, apart altogether from piece-work prices, and they must exert themselves to make it a condition that all those engaged upon piece-work shall be paid their fair share of the surplus through the pay-office, instead of through the piece-master. Should it be proved that members have connived at the introduction of piece-work, by not

making it known at the first Branch meeting after it has been stated that members are working by the piece, they shall be subject to such fine, not exceeding £2, as the Branch or Committee consider the case deserves, or to exclusion.

The United Journeymen Brassfounders, Turners, Fitters, and Finishers. Rule 16.

If piece-work or premium bonus is introduced by employers into shops which have hitherto worked day-work, and the members are discharged for refusing to work by piece, or premium bonus, they shall be entitled to association benefit. Members must consult the officers of their Branch before taking any definite action. If in a shop engaged in a dispute of this nature, there be two-thirds voting in favour of accepting piece-work, with the consent of their Branch, the same shall be considered binding on all members working in said shop. In Branches or shops where piece-work is established, the members must ascertain the prices of jobs before starting; the prices of all work to be generally made known to the members in the shop.

Bristol Brassfounders' and Finishers' Trade Society. Rule 44.

In any piece-work shop a list of prices paid shall be kept by all the men, and no member shall be allowed to work below such price.

No member or members shall either give a price for new work, or a new price for work already catalogued, without first obtaining the consent of the majority of the society men working in the same shop.

The penalty for breach of this rule shall be a fine or exclusion from this Society, as may be decided at a summoned meeting.

London Society of Amalgamated Brassworkers. Rule 28.

Any member asking for or taking work by contract or piece in any shop where the same does not at present exist, and the same being proved to the satisfaction of the Executive Committee, shall be fined £1 for the first offence, and for the second be expelled.

National Society of Coppersmiths, Braziers, and Metalworkers. Rule 33.

In all cases where employers seek to introduce conditions other than day-work, members must at once report same, with conditions proposed, to the Executive Council, whose consent must be obtained previous to accepting such work.

Whenever practicable piece-work, etc., shall be worked and shared collectively, the balance to be apportioned in the office, if possible, to each individual concerned on time worked and wages paid.

Any member being offered a job on piece-work, the bonus system, or any method of payment other than by the hour, day, or week; or should he be asked to quote a price or prices, or time limit for work to be done, shall, before taking the job or quoting prices, etc., consult the men working in the shop with the object of taking or giving, amending or rejecting such prices or time limit as will meet with their general approval. In all cases day-work rates must be guaranteed, and each job to stand by itself.

Any member starting or working in any shop or place where these conditions are not enforced or maintained, shall immediately inform the secretary in writing of same, and any member neglecting to do so, or working contrary to these conditions, shall be liable to a fine not exceeding £5; any member so fined to be suspended from all benefits until such fine is paid, and if not paid within three months the offending member shall be summoned before the

Executive Council to show cause why such fine should not be paid, and should no satisfactory explanation be given, he shall be expelled and not allowed to rejoin until such fine is paid.

ASSOCIATED BLACKSMITHS' AND IRON WORKERS' SOCIETY. Rule 24.

1. The members of the Society shall not encourage the working of overtime or piece-work; but where piece-work is established, and it is not possible to do away with it, a list of prices mutually agreed upon shall be fixed in each shop and known to all the members. It shall be the duty of every member to acquaint the shop delegate and the members generally with the prevailing price of piece-work being done, and to give any information which may be required for protecting such prices. Any member failing to comply with this Rule shall be fined in the sum of 5s. for each offence, or otherwise dealt with as the nature of the case may deserve.

2. It is laid down as a clear and distinct principle for the guidance of members on piece-work, that no member shall under any circumstances be permitted to sign a contract for any piece-work. Any member discovered acting in violation of this instruction will for the first offence be liable to be fined in any sum not exceeding £5 sterling, and for the second offence shall be liable to be expelled from this Society, forfeiting all claims upon its funds, or otherwise dealt with as the nature of the case deserves.

3. No member of the Society shall work more than one fire. Any member violating this instruction shall be fined £1 for the first offence, and for the second offence shall be liable to be expelled from the Society, or otherwise dealt with as the nature of the case deserves. Any members working piece-work in company must share out equally the money earned. No heating fire shall be used by any company of smiths, and no hammermen will be permitted to do heating work. Any member endeavouring directly or indirectly to injure any of his brethren, so as to reduce the value of their labour, or act in any way to injure the trade, he shall immediately be brought to account by the Branch, and be dealt with as the nature of the case deserves.

U.K. SOCIETY OF AMALGAMATED SMITHS AND STRIKERS. Rule 46.

1. It is not to the interests of this Society for members to look with favour on the piece-work system, neither is this rule to be considered as fostering the system in the slightest degree, but, on the contrary, the Society considers it to be a duty to check, as far as possible, the evils arising from the inequalities of the system whereby it becomes injurious to the members, and to prevent its introduction into any shop or district where it does not at present exist. It therefore becomes a duty for every member, as far as possible, to insist upon having a proper rate of wages guaranteed altogether apart from piece-work prices.

2. Any member asking for, or taking work by contract in any shop where piece-work does not previously exist, or any member taking work by contract and not sharing equally in proportion to his wages any surplus or balance earned over and above the weekly wages paid to members and other persons working on such job, on the same being proved to the satisfaction of the Branch, or District Committee, he shall be fined 10s. for the first offence, £1 for the second offence, and for the third offence be expelled from the Society, subject to the approval of the Executive Council.

3. Any Branch Committee (or in districts where there are two or more branches in close proximity to each other, District Committees) where piece-work is already established, shall be allowed to frame bye-laws to regulate their prices, and also to fix the amount members shall be allowed to earn over and above their rate of wages; such bye-laws, after having received the sanction of the Executive Council, shall render members eligible to Dispute Benefit under Rule 41; but in all cases of dispute each separate dispute must

receive the sanction of the Executive Council before members are entitled to receive Dispute Benefit.

4. Any member taking work by contract below the price fixed by the Branch or District Committees, thereby tending to bring about a reduction in the prices paid, shall be fined 10s. for the first offence, £1 for the second offence, and for the third offence shall be expelled from the Society, subject to the approval of the Executive Council.

5. Any member found to be using his influence to discharge, or cause to be discharged or suspended from his employment any man or men working on piece or contract jobs, who are in receipt of the ordinary rate of wages of the district, and substituting boy labour or cheaper labour in their places, for the purpose of making surpluses over and above the rate of wages of the district, shall be fined 10s. for the first offence, £1 for the second offence, and for the third offence shall be expelled from the Society. Branch Secretaries, where necessary, to supply the District Secretary with the facts of each case. Any member who is asked to accept a job on piece-work in the shop he is already employed in, at a reduced rate, without having received notice from the foreman of such reduction, shall be allowed to receive Dispute Benefit should he be discharged for refusing, provided he gives satisfactory reasons to his Branch Committee for such refusal.

Friendly Society of Ironfounders of England, Ireland, and Wales. Rule 35.

1. In the interests of the Society it is highly undesirable that our members should encourage any form of piece-work or bonus system; but where our members, with the consent of the Council, are working piece-work, they must strictly observe the following conditions.

2. Branches where piece-work or bonus system is done shall be allowed to frame bye-laws to protect their prices, which, when sanctioned by the Council, will be strictly binding on all the members working in the Branch.

3. Any member soliciting piece-work, or accepting same without the sanction of the Council, in any foundry where piece-work or bonus system did not previously exist, shall, upon the case being proved to the satisfaction of his Branch, be fined for the first offence the sum of 20s., for the second 40s., and for the third shall be expelled.

4. Any member accepting piece-work or bonus system below the usual price, or contrary to the Branch bye-laws, without sanction of the Council, shall be fined 20s. for the first offence, 40s. for the second, and for the third shall be expelled.

5. Any member taking piece-work or bonus system and not sharing equally with all the men engaged on the job any surplus of price, shall be fined 20s. for the first offence, 40s. for the second, and for the third shall be expelled.

6. All cases of dispute arising under this rule must be sanctioned by the Council before the members are entitled to Dispute Benefit.

Associated Ironmoulders of Scotland. Rule 40.

1. No member or members shall be allowed, either directly or indirectly, to encourage the establishment of piece-work; but, where it has already been established, they shall, by every legitimate means, endeavour to have it abolished.

2. Any member employed by the day and ordered to go on by the piece, must oppose such order as far as lies in his power; should he require to leave his employment, or be discharged through this cause, he shall receive benefit if otherwise entitled.

3. Members commencing to work by the piece, and finding, after a fair trial, the price given will not enable them to earn an average day's pay, will receive benefit if leaving on this account, with the sanction of the shop and

Committee, should they be otherwise entitled ; and no member can commence afterwards to said job without the sanction of District Committee, who shall alone have the power to open or shut said job, or to grant or decline benefit in any case.

4. The members employed in piece-work shops shall draw up a code of bye-laws for the regulation of prices, a copy of which must be left with the secretary of the district for reference in cases of reduction in prices, or any dispute about the quantity of work done ; and any alteration in prices, either in the form of an advance or reduction, must be promptly reported to the secretary by shop delegate—who in turn will report to Central Office—under a penalty of 1s.

5. Members working by the piece and commencing on a new job, are strictly enjoined to have the price fixed within three days after commencing ; and, failing to obtain a satisfactory agreement within that time, will receive benefit on leaving if otherwise entitled to it. Any member out on a disputed job to have the first chance to return to the job.

6. Members are strictly enjoined to dispense with the employment of assistants altogether. No member of this Society to have more than one assistant or apprentice, and then only when absolutely necessary.

7. Apprentices are instructed to refuse or encourage any form of piece-work ; and in refusing to work any job by the piece he shall, if discharged, be entitled to receive benefit as per Apprentice Rule. No apprentice can take a job by piece which has been refused by a former apprentice, under a penalty of 5s.

Amalgamated Society of Coremakers. Rule 54.

1. It is essential in the interest of our members in general that piece-work should be discouraged in any form whatever. But cases do arise where our members are compelled by force of circumstances to work under a system of piece-work. It is therefore necessary that the following Rules should be observed.

2. In branches where our members are working piece-work the Committee shall formulate a set of bye-laws to govern and protect the prices paid to our members, such bye-laws to be submitted to the Council, and when sanctioned by them they will be strictly binding on all our members working in the branch.

3. Any member asking for or taking work by piece or contract in any shop or foundry where such a system has not previously been in vogue (unless by sanction of the Council) shall, on the same being proved to the satisfaction of the Council, be fined a sum not exceeding 20s. for the first offence, 40s. for the second offence, and should the member again commit himself he will be excluded.

4. It shall be imperative on all members working piece-work that they shall be paid through the office of the firm, and that each member shall be guaranteed apart altogether from piece prices the minimum wage of the district. Violation of this Rule will subject the offending member to a fine not exceeding £1 at the discretion of the Branch Committee.

5. Any member found to be using his influence to obtain the discharge or suspension of any other member working piece-work with an idea of substituting boy or other cheap labour in his place so as to increase the surplus over the minimum rate of wage for the remainder, such member shall be fined £1 for the first offence, £2 for the second, and for the third expelled.

6. Should any member receive an intimation from his foreman or employer that it is their intention to place him on piece-work, he shall inform the Branch Secretary of the fact within 24 hours or be fined 5s. The Secretary to call the Committee together to consider the matter. They shall take such steps as they in their judgment consider best, first to prevent, if possible, the introduction of piece-work in any form, and failing to do so, they shall see that a fair price is fixed for the work to be done that will enable our members to earn

a fair wage without injury to themselves. The terms to be submitted to the Council for approval before being accepted.

7. Should any member commence work under any system of piece-work without first receiving the consent of the Council through his Branch he will incur a fine of 20s. and 5s. per day for every day he may work previous to the sanction of the Council being given.

8. Any member taking a job at a less price than has previously been paid, or taking a job and not sharing equally with all our members engaged on the same work, he will be fined 20s. for the first offence, 40s. for the second, and for the third offence he shall be expelled.

9. Should it be proved to the satisfaction of the Branch Committee that any member has directly or indirectly encouraged or solicited or induced any other member to solicit the introduction of piece-work of any kind, the said member will incur a penalty of 20s. for the first offence, 40s. for the second, and for the third he will be excluded.

10. Branch Committees are empowered to withdraw any member of the Branch under these Rules and grant them donation according to Rule.

Associated Iron, Steel, and Brass Dressers of Scotland. Rule 64.

No member of this Association shall have power to establish piece-work directly or indirectly, but shall, so far as may be in his power, endeavour to get it abolished. Any member violating this clause shall be expelled. But where piece-work is unfortunately established, members are at liberty to work in said shops, and they may also compete for the position of piece-master in said shops. But in no case can a piece-master become or remain a member of this Association while employed in the shop in which he has established piece-work.

General Iron Fitters' Association. Rule 17, Section 2.

2. Any member being discharged through refusing to take a job below the price set on it by the men working in the same shop, or work below the established day wage of the district, or withdrawn by a decision of the Executive Council, shall be entitled to receive support.

Rule 18, Section 2.

2. A member or members knowingly taking a job at a lower rate than that fixed by the members working in the same shop, accepting, or offering to accept, piece-work which has been done on day's time without the consent of the Executive Council, or work at a rate under the established day's wage of that district, or working against the advice of the Executive Council, shall be fined any sum the Executive Council may determine, or be expelled from the Union.

United Society of Boilermakers and Iron and Steel Shipbuilders. Rule 34.

When members are compelled to work piece-work, and it be proved to the satisfaction of the District Committee and approved of by the Executive Council that the employer or employers are reducing the prices below the usual and reasonable prices, they shall allow the members resisting the reduction the following: 12s. per week for eight weeks. They shall after signing the vacant books three consecutive days be entitled to commence donation on the fourth day. Any member or members leaving their employment under this section must inform the Executive Council, through their secretary, of the same within three days from the time of leaving, or lose the benefit for the time they neglect. All arrears must be deducted before any monies are paid to the members. Members discharged for refusing to submit to a reduction shall receive the benefit of this rule.

SHEET IRON WORKERS' AND LIGHT PLATERS' SOCIETY. Rule 32.

1. No member shall either directly or indirectly encourage the establishment of piece-work, but where it has already been established they shall by every legitimate means endeavour to have it abolished.

2. Any member accepting a piece-work job at a price another member has refused to do it for, or in any other way trying to cut down the prices for piece-work, shall be brought before his Branch, and, if found guilty, shall be fined in a sum not exceeding 15s.

3. Members employed in a shop where piece-work is wrought, shall draw up a code of bye-laws for the regulation of prices, and a copy shall be forwarded to the Branch Secretary by the shop steward.

4. Members are enjoined to dispense altogether with the employment of boys as assistants.

SCOTTISH TINPLATE, BRAZIERS, AND SHEET METAL WORKERS' SOCIETY. Rule 29.

That no member shall commence or resume the system of working by the piece on any job without first consulting the office-bearers, who shall bring the case before the Committee, and should any member be allowed to work by the piece and be required to work overtime or on the holidays, he shall charge time-and-half.

BIRMINGHAM OPERATIVE TINPLATE, SHEET METAL WORKERS, AND BRAZIERS' SOCIETY. Rule 27.

Any article introduced into any manufactory, not previously priced, shall be priced by a majority of members working in the shop, or by a committee of members, and no price shall be recognised except in accordance with this Rule. The shop steward shall enter the same in a book (kept by him for that purpose and provided by the Society), failing which he shall be liable to any fine not exceeding 5s. the Executive Committee shall deem fit. The members of the General Committee, working in their respective manufactories, shall see to the carrying out of the same, or be liable to the same penalties as shop stewards.

GALVANISED HOLLOW-WARE, SHEET METAL WORKERS, AND BRAZIERS' ASSOCIATION. Rule 27.

1. Any member of this Association having a new article to make shall, before commencing it, call his shopmates together in the same line of work, who shall put a fair price on the article in question, and it shall be the duty of the men to see that such prices, when they are obtained, are duly entered in the price book by the collector, who shall take charge of the same for the convenience of the men, and forward a copy of the particulars to the General Office for confirmation by the E.C. or otherwise.

2. Should the price agreed upon by the members in the shop be disputed by the employer or manager, no member shall be allowed to make the article *only under protest*, until the E.C. have had an opportunity of considering same and fixing a price. Their decision on such matters to be final.

3. Any member neglecting to call his shopmates together, as specified in this Rule, shall be fined 2s. 6d. for each offence, and any member not attending such meeting when called upon shall be fined 1s.

NATIONAL AMALGAMATED LOCK, LATCH, AND KEYMAKERS' TRADE SOCIETY. Rule 30.

Any member of this Society, pricing any work in question, shall call a committee of his shopmates in the same line of work, who shall put a fair price on the work in question, and it shall be the duty of the shop secretary to see that such prices, when they are obtained, are duly entered in the price book, to be kept by him for the convenience of the men. Any member neglecting to call a committee, as specified in this Rule, if necessary, shall be brought before a Branch Committee for investigation, and if any member makes such new articles, and the price, put on it by the Committee, is disputed by the master or foreman, the member shall not make it or draw money upon such said work in dispute, but shall state the case before the officers of the Society, who shall be empowered to lend him money from the trade funds until such work in dispute is amicably settled, and as soon as he receives the money for the said work, he must refund it to the Society.

CHAIN MAKERS' AND STRIKERS' ASSOCIATION. Rule 22.

If a member is more than 6s. in arrears, or leaves the chain trade, or should he go to work in any factory or shop in the trade where this Association is inoperative, he shall cease to be a member, but he shall be allowed to re-enter the Association by obtaining the consent of the Executive Council, after returning to work in any factory or shop where this Association is in operation. Further, no member of this Association shall sign a contract or agreement to work for an employer any stipulated length of time that is contrary to the custom of the trade ; neither shall he agree to work for any list of prices not recognised as the standard prices of the trade, without first getting the consent of the Executive Council. Any member doing so, or acting contrary to this Rule, will be expelled and forfeit all claims on this Association.

AMALGAMATED ANVIL AND VICE MAKERS' ASSOCIATION. Rule 28.

Any workman or workmen desirous of raising the question of prices for special work may bring their case before the Executive Council, through their delegates, who shall have power to decide in every case. In the event of a dispute between members and their employer, all members must have the sanction of the Executive Council before giving notice to leave their situations. Only those who have been on strike six clear working days shall receive strike pay. The Executive Council shall have power to make grants should they think the circumstances of sufficient importance to do so.

NATIONAL UNION OF OPERATIVE HEATING AND DOMESTIC ENGINEERS. Rule 18.

1. No member shall be allowed to enter into any contract with his employer or any person to carry on work by the piece, nor shall he be a party to cultivate the system in any shop where the same has never existed. In the event of any member starting to work in a firm where the system has been carried on, and called upon to work by the piece, he shall be remunerated in accordance with the local conditions.

2. No member shall be permitted to take work at a lower rate than the prices previously acknowledged in the shop or job unless with the full knowledge and consent of the Branch.

3. The penalty for infringement of any of these sections shall be :

For the first offence, not to exceed £1.
For the second offence, not to exceed £5.
For third offence, suspension from all benefits for two years.

APPENDIX C

PIECE-WORK RULES AND AGREEMENTS IN THE WOOD-WORKING AND BUILDING TRADES

THE following are a few selected rules and agreements applying to the woodworking and building trades. The Societies in these trades are in almost all cases strongly opposed to all forms of payment by results, and it should be noted that, even where piece-work agreements exist, there are, as a rule, very few members working under the system, at least in organised districts. The vast majority of woodworking and building workers are time-workers.

WOODWORKING TRADES

AMALGAMATED SOCIETY OF CARPENTERS AND JOINERS. Rule 48, Clause 1.

It shall be competent for any M.C., D.C., B.C., or Branch at a special or quarterly meeting, to fine or expel any member from the Society upon satisfactory proof being given that such member has refused to comply with their decision, or by his conduct brought the Society into discredit, wilfully violated the recognised trade rules of the district in which he is working, or working on a co-partnership system, when such system makes provision for the operatives holding only a minority of the shares in the concern, taking a sub-contract or piece-work, or working for either of these classes of employers (sub-contractor or piece-worker being defined as a person taking the labour of a job only, and not supplying the material), or fixing, using, or finishing work which has been made under unfair conditions, either in the United Kingdom or abroad, or contrary to the recognised trade rules of the district in which it has been prepared, or has fraudulently received or misapplied the funds of the Society, or the moneys of any member or candidate entrusted to him for payment to the Society.

GENERAL UNION OF OPERATIVE CARPENTERS AND JOINERS. Rule 31.

Any member proved to the satisfaction of the E.C., District Committee, or Lodge to be working against the interests of the Society by working on the Premium Bonus System, or taking piece-work, or sub-contracting (sub-contracting and piece-work being defined as taking the labour of a job and not supplying the material), or working for either class of employer, or fixing or using work which has been made under unfair conditions or contrary to the recognised trade rules of the district in which it has been made, may be fined or expelled as the E.C., District Committee, or Lodge may determine. Should any member be fined under this or any other Rule where no fine is fixed, such fine not to exceed £1.

National Amalgamated Furnishing Trades' Association.
Rule 44 (Clause B).

A member knowingly taking a job at a lower price than that fixed by the members working in the same shop, accepting, or offering to accept piece or lump work in an established and exclusive day-work shop, or working under the established day wages of that town, or going to work in a shop where the men have been withdrawn by the advice of the Executive Committee, shall, on its being proved, be fined such sum not exceeding £2, or be expelled, as the members at the next meeting of his Branch shall decide, subject to an appeal to a summoned meeting of his Branch. If dissatisfied with the decision of the summoned meeting, he may appeal to the Executive Committee, but must give notice to the General Secretary within one week.

Glasgow and District Furniture Trades' Federation

Conditions of Settlement I. Rules 1 and 2.

Conditions of Settlement mutually adjusted and agreed upon between the Scottish Furniture Manufacturers' Association and the United Furniture Trades' Association, January 1899, revised June 30, 1914.

1. *Piece-work.*—It shall be in the option of the employers to adopt the system of piece-work on repeat work or time-work as they prefer. It must be clearly understood that by repeat work is meant ordinary stock jobs or catalogue work, or patterns or designs commonly and repeatedly made in the workshop, or any new work after it has been made three times on day wages by the average man. The employer or his representatives, in conjunction with the workmen employed by him in the particular department of the workshop affected, shall mutually arrange the prices.

The Scottish Furniture Manufacturers' Association will not permit any of its members to impose any piece-work conditions which will not allow a workman of average efficiency to earn at least the wage at which he is rated.

It shall also be in the discretion of the employers and the workmen to arrange prices for repeat work upon which any alteration of a minor character may be made.

Employers will be held responsible for any inefficient work which may be done by any person other than the workman who has taken out the job by the piece, or for bad material or any time lost waiting for material, and shall pay the workman thus affected for all time lost, over and above the fixed price of the said job. The condition of the material must be at once intimated to the employer or his representatives. In the event of a piece job being required by the employer in less than the usual average time taken for such a job, and thus necessitating the employment of extra workmen on the said job, the employer will be held responsible for any extra cost resulting therefrom, thus ensuring that the workman who has taken out the job shall not lose thereby. Provided always that the employer, for the causes stated, or for any other cause, requiring to put additional men on the piece-work job, the value of the work done on said job shall then be assessed by the employer or his representatives and the workmen in the particular department, and the job shall then be completed on day wages. All fitting up to be done on day wages unless otherwise stipulated.

2. *Restriction.*—There shall be no restriction or undue pressure imposed on the time output of the workmen, nor shall the skill of any man be hampered in any way by either party.

HIGH WYCOMBE AND DISTRICT FURNISHING TRADES' ASSOCIATION. Working Rules 5 and 6.

5. *Piece-work.*—The price of piece-work jobs shall be adjusted upon the basis of the standard rates of wages paid to fully qualified journeymen mechanics.

6. Employers reserve to themselves the right to employ any employee on piece or day work in any department.

BIRMINGHAM FURNISHING TRADES' AGREEMENT. Clauses (3) and (4).

(3) In shops where the piece-work system obtains price lists to be advanced to make it possible for an average man to earn eightpence halfpenny (8½d.) per hour up to a limit of 10 per cent (10%) advance.

(4) In all shops an advance of 5 per cent (5%) shall be paid on existing price lists.

LONDON JOINT COMMITTEE OF COACHMAKERS, WHEELWRIGHTS, AND MOTOR BUILDERS. Rule 6.

In all cases when employers seek to introduce piece-work conditions, where hitherto such conditions have not been established, members must at once report same, with conditions proposed, to the officers of their Union who shall report to this Committee, whose consent must be obtained before members be allowed to accept piece-work.

(*a*) In all cases day-work rates must be guaranteed, irrespective of piece-work prices.

(*b*) Piece-work shall be worked collectively, balances to be apportioned and paid to each individual by the office on time worked and wages paid.

UNITED KINGDOM SOCIETY OF COACHMAKERS. Rule 65.

Section 3.—Any pieceman not sharing balance with his workmen, according to their wages, shall be fined a sum not exceeding 20s. at the discretion of the Committee.

Section 4.—No pieceman shall employ any man under the standard wages of the pieceman's shop, which must not be less than the standard rate of wages of town, he shall produce his book when required by Town Committee, or be fined not exceeding 20s. All wages and balances to be paid through the office.

Section 6.—Bodymakers working piece-work shall claim the right to deface, or obliterate their cantboards after using, if they think fit, providing it is made in their own time and they have not been paid for it.

OTHER BUILDING TRADES

LIVERPOOL AND BIRKENHEAD OPERATIVE SHIP AND HOUSE PAINTERS' BENEFIT ASSOCIATION. Rule 22.

That no member of this Association shall be allowed to undertake any sub-contracts from any employers engaged in the trade (except masts and yards), to the exclusion of other members being employed in the usual way by the day, under a penalty of 20s. for each day he may be engaged on such sub-contract, or be expelled from the Association as the Committee may determine. Any member knowingly working with a sub-contractor shall be fined any sum not exceeding 20s., as the Committee may think fit to inflict.

SOCIETY OF OPERATIVE STONEMASONS OF ENGLAND AND WALES. Rule 12, Section 2.

Lodges harassed by piece-work or sub-contracting may apply at a reasonable time for a grant to abolish it. Where sub-contracting or piece-work is abolished, such is binding with the Society.

SCOTTISH ASSOCIATION PAVIORS' FEDERAL UNION. Rule 7.

No foreman or pavior can be a member of this Society who will make any engagement or private agreement with any corporation, company, or paving contractor, or take sub-contracts from them directly or indirectly, under no less a penalty than the members of the Branch to which he belongs may see proper to inflict.

APPENDIX D

"POOLING" AND COLLECTIVE PIECE-WORK

THE first of the following documents is a typical scheme, drawn up by the employers for a large engineering works and providing for the pooling of piece-work balances. It illustrates the working of a limited system of "pooling," in which the "pool" is confined to a particular trade.

The second document contains the piece-work provisions of the 1913 Agreement between the Unions in the Yorkshire dyeing trade and the Bradford Dyers' Association; while the third document is a specimen agreement for collective piece-work on a "squad" basis, taken from the dyeing trade of Yorkshire.

Both documents illustrate Chapter II.

I

POOLING OF PIECE-WORK BALANCES

Rules

1. That members shall pool all balances of piece-work, viz.: fitters with fitters, planers with planers, drillers with drillers, and turners and universal grinders will pool together in each department.

2. That one workman shall be appointed in each department, whose duty it shall be to control the pooling, and each week every man must produce his wage ticket, and state the number of hours he has worked in that week, to the man in charge of the pool.

3. No workman shall be entitled to pool until he has worked in the works four weeks.

4. That one workman shall be elected from each department of the works to form the Works Committee, and when formed they shall elect a Chairman and Secretary.

5. That each workman shall contribute one penny per month, the same to cover expenses incurred by the Works Committee.

6. That a GENERAL SHOPS MEETING shall be held every six months, at which the Committee and a Treasurer shall be elected, the same to hold office during the following six months. In the event of a vacancy taking place on the Committee, or in the Treasurership, the Committee shall have power to call an interim General Meeting to fill the vacancy, or appoint a workman to fill the position *pro tempore*.

7. That a Minute Book shall be obtained, in which shall be entered a correct record of the proceedings of each meeting.

8. That each workman is expected to possess a copy of these Rules, which will be supplied on the payment of one penny per copy.

9. That no worker shall be allowed to attend the shops meetings who is under 18 years of age.

10. Any workman having a grievance must inform the shop steward of his department, who will submit it to the Committee at their next meeting.

11. All Members not attending a shops meeting when notified of same, shall be fined the sum of sixpence unless a satisfactory reason can be given. Any Member violating these Rules shall be dealt with in the first instance by the Workshop Committee, and in the event of the member still refusing to comply with these Rules, the Workshop Committee shall then remit the case, stating full particulars to the Branch or District Committee of the Society to which the workman belongs.

CLAUSES FROM THE AGREEMENT between the Bradford Dyers' Association, Ltd., and the National Society of Dyers, the Amalgamated Society of Dyers, and the Gas Workers' and General Labourers' Union.

Collective Piece-work.

6. The Association may at any Branch introduce payment by piece-work rates. All piece-work shall be based on collective work and collective payment. By collective piece-work is meant work performed by sets or groups of employees.

7. The fixing of rates and the arrangement of sets shall be mutually agreed upon in writing by representatives of the Association and the Unions. Such rates shall be so fixed as to enable a full-rated man to earn not less than 7d. per hour. At any branch introducing piece-work, it shall be a condition of the introduction that every employee (including females) engaged on productive work shall be paid on a piece-work basis within one month from the commencement of the trial.

8. No rate or set shall be altered without the consent in writing of the Association and the Union or Unions to which the employees affected belong.

9. Trials of three calendar months' duration shall precede the final settlement of rates.

10. During the three months' trial the remuneration of those engaged on the trial shall not be less than the day rates payable under this agreement.

11. If after twelve calendar months from the establishment of the final rates for collective piece-work, the employees at any Branch so decide they shall have the right, upon giving three calendar months' notice in writing, to revert to payment of wages on hourly rates.

12. The rates of employees who on February 20, 1913, were engaged on piece-work shall as from that date be increased where necessary, so as to enable a full-rated man to earn not less than 7d. per hour.

13. In addition to the rates of payment fixed upon for piece-workers, each employee shall, when engaged on night turn, receive 1s. 6d. per night extra, but no other allowance.

14. There shall, as based on the census of January 1, 1913, be no material displacement of adult labour consequent on or due to the introduction of piece-work, but the Association shall have full liberty subject to Clauses 7 and 8, to transfer labour between its various branches, and in the meantime any displacement of labour shall so far as possible be that of boys, to help to meet which the engagement of boy labour shall be temporarily stopped. After the adjustment so provided the Association shall be entitled to reinstate boy and other labour on the same basis as hitherto.

15. From and after the 1st July 1913, no employee shall, unless by mutual agreement between the Union to which he belongs and the Association, be required to work after 12 noon on Saturdays, and an employee on night turn not, unless by mutual agreement between the Association and the Union to which he belongs, work more than five nights in any week, and he shall cease

work not later than 6 A.M. each day, except where work on a continuous process is continued because the day employees are late.

16. Clause 15 shall not apply to cleaning up or to processes necessary to putting the goods into a condition of safety, *e.g.* drying, which may be carried on until 3 o'clock P.M. on Saturdays. Piece-workers shall be entitled to extra payment at the rate of 3½d. per hour after 6 P.M., and 12 noon on Saturdays.

17. The Association may at any time not less than one month after the commencement of a piece-work trial elect to demonstrate as to the sufficiency of any rate or rates to enable the men without excessive physical strain to earn not less than 7d. per hour. The demonstration shall be conducted by the workmen engaged on the machine to which the demonstration is to apply, and during such demonstration the employees shall work in the manner directed by the Association. If after such demonstration agreement is not arrived at in regard to the piece-work rate or rates, the matter shall be referred to the Reference Board as provided in Clause 18 of this Agreement.

18. If the Association fail to satisfy the representatives of the Union of the sufficiency of any rate or of the fairness of the conditions the question shall be referred to the Reference Board for decision, and if the Association fails to demonstrate that the rate is sufficient or that the conditions are fair (as the case may be), then the Association shall forthwith increase the rate or alter the conditions as the case may require.

MEMORANDUM OF ARRANGEMENT GOVERNING THE INTRODUCTION OF COLLECTIVE PIECE-WORK AT A DYE WORKS

1. That all piece-work shall be based on collective work and collective payment.

2. By collective piece-work is meant payment for work performed by groups of employees.

3. The fixing of rates and the agreements of sets shall be mutually agreed upon by representatives of the firm and the workmen.

4. That no rate or set once agreed upon shall be altered without the consent in writing of both parties to the arrangement.

5. That it shall be a condition of the introduction of piece-work that every employee, including females, engaged on productive work shall be paid on a piece-work basis within three months from the date of commencement of the trial.

6. That no workman on piece-work shall, unless by mutual consent between the Union and the firm, be required to work after 12 noon on Saturdays, and that workmen employed on night turn shall not, unless by mutual agreement between the Union and the firm, work more than five nights in any week, and they shall cease work not later than 6 A.M. each day.

7. That an undertaking be required from the firm that they will guarantee that not less than day-rates are earned during the trial and until the settlement of the piece-rates.

8. That all existing extra payments and allowances for night work shall be abolished, and in lieu thereof, each worker commencing on a piece-work trial shall be paid 1s. 6d. per night extra.

9. That for all time worked after the usual stopping time, whether day or night, overtime rates shall be paid at the rate of an additional payment of 3½d. per hour.

10. *Broad and Narrow Work.* Narrow goods shall be regarded as goods under 40 inches, and broad goods shall be regarded as goods of 40 inches and over.

FACTORY AND WORKSHOP ACT: PARTICULARS OF PIECE-WORK

Wet Stentering pooled with Calendering, Belt-Stretching, Folding, Making-up, and Warehouse

The duties of the employees in these sets are to keep all machinery clean and well oiled and the belts in good order, all duties in connection with the producing of the goods to be done in a satisfactory manner. The Department to be kept clean and orderly.

The Rates of Pay will be as follows:

Wet Stentering	3s. 10½d.	per 100 pieces of 30 yards
Calendering and Belt-Stretching .	9d.	,, ,, ,,
Folding	7d.	,, ,, ,,
Warehouse	5½d.	,, ,, ,,

The ordinary sets will consist of the following persons and their hour rates:

Men: 1 at 4½d.; 4 at 4½d.; 16 at 5d.
Boys: 1 at 2¾d.
Women and Girls: 12 at 2½d.; 6 at 2¾d.; 11 at 2¾d.; 5 at 1½d.

Production.—The production for the wet stentering will be taken from recorders, and for the calendering, folding, and warehouse, from pieces folded off folding machine.

The amount earned will be pooled and divided among the sets in proportion to their hour rates and the hours worked.

Any assistance required by the sets must be paid for by the sets.

A piece-work trial for eight weeks, in accordance with the above details, will commence on Wednesday December 18, 1912, and during this trial the firm guarantee that no one will draw less than their hour rate of wages.

APPENDIX E

THE PREMIUM BONUS SYSTEM

The following four documents illustrate the working of the Premium Bonus System in this country. The first is a copy of a short explanatory leaflet circulated in an important works on the introduction of the scheme. The second is the Carlisle Memorandum, agreed upon by the Engineering Employers' Federation and the Amalgamated Society of Engineers in 1902, which is still the only national agreement regulating the system. The third document contains the rules for the working of the system drawn up by the Barrow-in-Furness engineers in 1909, while the fourth is a copy of the agreement under which disputes are now dealt with in Barrow, where the system is in almost general operation.

I

PREMIUM BONUS SYSTEM

This system has been introduced in America with great success as the only solution of the twofold problem to reduce cost of production concurrently with increasing the wage of the worker.

It is considered that in introducing this system at the Linotype Factory, Broadheath, it will do away with the abuses of the present Piece-work System, and be satisfactory to all concerned.

The principle on which it is worked is as follows :

A basis time will be established for every job in the shop, and this time will be so fixed that any man of average skill will be easily able to accomplish the job within it.

The time for the job once having been fixed will never be changed unless the job, or method of executing it, or the machine on which it is done, is changed.

When the job is done in less than this basis time, he will be paid for the *time saved* at half his time-rate.

It is quite clear that, if an average man can execute the job within the basis time when first starting the work, with practice he will soon be able to lessen that time considerably, and as the example below shows, his weekly wage can be very considerably increased. In any case, every man will receive his *time wage as a minimum*, and as it is intended to fix the *basis times* on a *liberal scale*, it is expected that it will be exceptional if any one working on a job on which the time has been fixed does not make a considerable premium. It will be to the firm's interest as well as to the man's interest that every man shall earn a premium; for, as the time is reduced, the cost of the job to the firm is diminished ; and it is for this reason that a *basis time* can be fixed that shall *never be altered*, except under conditions mentioned in a previous paragraph.

Below is an example of how the System will work in practice :

Let us suppose the basis time for a job be fixed at one hour. Suppose a man to be employed at 36s. per week—roughly, his pay comes out at 8d. per hour. As the man becomes familiar with the work, supposing that he takes —instead of one hour—thirty-five minutes, he would be paid for thirty-five minutes at his time-rate, *i.e.* at 8d. per hour, and for twenty-five minutes (the time saved) at 4d. per hour. He would therefore receive for thirty-five minutes' work, pay at the rate of 10·855d. per hour. In a week occupied with this job, or a series of similar jobs, he would have raised his pay from 36s. per week to 48s. ; and, as *there is no limit to the increased pay that he may draw, there is no reason why (with increased experience in the work) his pay should not far exceed even this amount.*

In factories in America where this system has been introduced, it is by no means unusual for the men to draw premiums amounting to an increase of 60 per cent on their wages.

II

THE PREMIUM BONUS SYSTEM

MEMORANDUM OF DECISION in Central Conference between the EXECUTIVE of the ENGINEERING EMPLOYERS' FEDERATION and the EXECUTIVE COUNCIL of the AMALGAMATED SOCIETY OF ENGINEERS, held at Carlisle, August 19 and 20, 1902.

1. That the employers' representatives should convey the terms of the following memorandum to the members of the Federation ; and
2. That the representatives of the A.S.E. should, on the other hand, remove all restrictions to the working of a bonus system in federated workshops.

MEMORANDUM REFERRED TO

The employers' representatives have not the power to settle the conditions which should be observed in connection with the working of a bonus system, without having previously obtained authority from the Federation in proper form.

They are, however, prepared to advise all employers who wish to establish such a system in the meantime to adopt the following suggestions :

1. The time-rate of wages (for each job) should in all cases be paid.
2. Overtime and nightshifts to be paid on the same conditions as already prevail in each workshop.
3. A time limit, after it has been established, should only be changed if the method or means of manufacture are changed.
4. No firm should establish the bonus system without intending to adhere to it.

On behalf of the Engineering Employers' Federation,

(*Signed*) ALEX. SIEMENS—*Chairman.*

On behalf of the Amalgamated Society of Engineers,

(*Signed*) ALFRED SELLICKS—*Chairman.*
GEORGE N. BARNES—*Secretary.*

August 20, 1902.

III

LOCAL RULES REGULATING THE PREMIUM BONUS SYSTEM

A.S.E., S.E.M., U.M.W.A., BARROW-IN-FURNESS, JANUARY 1909.

It has now been deemed advisable that some bye-laws should be drawn up for the guidance of members working under the Premium Bonus System in this district. The clauses contained in this memorandum are the accepted terms.

1. The time-rate of wages (for each job) should in all cases be paid.
2. Overtime and nightshift to be paid on the same conditions as already prevail in each workshop for time-work.
3. A time limit, after it has been established, should only be changed if the method or means of manufacture are changed.
4. No firm should establish the Bonus System without intending to adhere to it.

The only clause that has or is likely to be prolific of dispute is the third clause. It is open to abuse from employer and employee alike.

Recording Time.

We consider it absolutely necessary for all members to keep a record of the details and time given for each operation.

Each operation should be confined to its own merits on the time given.

Alteration of Time Basis.

1. Any alteration of time through alteration of method must in all cases be reported by members to their secretary, and transferred from him to joint secretary for reference.

2. No alteration in time can be considered just which does not increase or decrease in equitable proportion to the labour or time required for such operation in comparison with the original basis.

Transfer of Work.

1. In the event of work being transferred from one department to another, we consider it a duty incumbent on members of the joint Societies to supply all information to each other concerning the same.

2. This can reasonably be done without trespass in any way on employer's time.

General.

As the system is intended to confer benefits to employer and employed, there can be no reason for secrecy on either side, if the system is to be regarded as just and impartial.

The mere change of drawings or order number of any job does not warrant reduction in established basis, but should be conducted in conformity with clauses bearing on alterations in this circular.

Unless the conditions herein expressed are strictly complied with, and all changes made in harmony with established times, members will be held in future as acting against the principles guiding the joint Unions in the working of the system.

IV

BARROW JOINT ENGINEERING TRADES

PROCEDURE TO BE OBSERVED IN CONNECTION WITH THE ADJUSTMENT OF PREMIUM BONUS BASIS TIMES

Clause 1.—Where the job to be performed is the same as on previous occasions, and the means or method of production has not been changed, the basis time allowed shall be the recognised time for the job. Recognised times shall not be reduced unless the means or method of production has been changed.

Clause 2.—Where the work to be performed is not the same or where the means or method of production has been changed, or where the job is one which has not previously been performed on Premium Bonus System, or one where there is no recognised basis time for the job, the rate-fixer, having seen the job and taken out an estimate of the time to be occupied on the job, will, as soon as possible after the job has been given out, see the workman or workmen who are to perform the work, and give any explanations that may be desired regarding the time allowed. The intention is that the least possible time should be occupied in putting the workman in the position of knowing what his basis time is for the job he is undertaking. The firm agree to make the necessary arrangements to ensure this.

Clause 3.—Basis times for new jobs shall be fixed having regard to the capacity of a workman of average ability. It is recognised that in the case of a new job the workman may be unable to carry out the work as expeditiously as on repeat jobs. To meet this, the firm agree, on the first job, an allowance may be made to the workman should the necessities of the case require this. Such allowance shall be based on the average earnings of the workman concerned for the previous month.

Clause 4.—In the event of the workman taking exception to the time allowed, the rate-fixer shall endeavour to convince him of the sufficiency of the time. Should he not succeed, he shall refer the matter to the chief rate-fixer for his opinion, and thereafter again see the workman in accordance therewith.

Clause 5.—Failing settlement between the rate-fixers and the workman, the question shall be referred by the rate-fixer to the Appeals Section of the Rate-fixing Department. In order that the claim of the workman may be considered, a form will be supplied to the workman on which he shall state his claim, and hand the form to the representatives to be appointed under Clause 7 hereof, who shall thereafter submit the claim to the Appeals Section in accordance with this procedure. Meantime the job shall be proceeded with. Settlements regarding basis times shall be retrospective to the commencement of the job on which the question is raised, and shall be final and binding on all concerned.

Clause 6.—Complaints shall be dealt with by the Appeals Section in their order of priority.

Clause 7.—For the purpose of discussion of appeals lodged, two representatives shall be chosen from their own number by each trade in each main department of the works, who shall be authorised by the workman to confer with the Appeals Section of the Rate-fixing Department (composed of two officials of the firm) on questions affecting the trade and department they represent. For example, on a turning question in the Howitzer Department, two turners from that department would confer with the Appeals Section, and similarly in fitting questions two fitters would confer with the Appeals Section. The representative appointed in the terms of this Clause shall be given facilities, if desired, for examining cards and records relating to any question referred to them.

Clause 8.—The rate-fixer and the workman concerned may, if desired, be called upon to give evidence.

Clause 9.—Failing settlement being arrived at in the proceedings before the Appeals Section, the question may be referred, without further argument, to the Directors for decision.

Clause 10.—The foregoing procedure shall be followed in the case of claims for allowance over or above the basis time stated on the job card, and also in cases where in the execution of the job it is necessary to make further estimates of the work to be done.

Clause 11.—A portion of the job card containing the principal particulars relating to the job and the basis time shall be detachable and may be retained by the workman, if desired.

Clause 12. Detailed Pay-lines.—Pay-lines shall be given on which shall be inserted particulars of the total time worked, the bonus earned, and the allowances and deductions applicable to the pay to which the pay-line refers. A copy of the pay-line shall be given to each workman along with his pay, and shall be retained by him.

Workmen shall be paid on time check, but the firm on failure to return cards and after warning the workmen concerned, shall be entitled, pending return of the card, to withhold payment of wages due.

APPENDIX F

PRICE LISTS

I HAVE before me a number of typical piece-work price lists. Two short lists are reproduced in full as an indication of their general character. These are, first, a colliery list for Number 4 Seam at an important South Wales colliery, where most of the work is done piece-work, and secondly, a recent list from the boot and shoe industry " for lasting and finishing the British Army ankle boot." Short as these lists are, in comparison with the more complicated lists in many trades, they will serve to indicate the general character of piece-work " statements " agreed to between employers and Trade Unions. A list of a few of the other lists before me is appended with a view to giving some indication of the variety in existence.

I

SCHEDULE OF PRICES PAYABLE FOR DEAD AND OTHER WORK WHEN PROPERLY AND SATISFACTORILY PERFORMED IN THE WORKING OF No. 4 SEAM, STANDARD 1915.

	Description of Work.	s.	d.	*Rate.*
CUTTING	Cutting Large Clean Coal . . .	2	4	per ton
	Note.—The price paid for Large Coal covers the price of any small sent out in the trams with the Large Coal.			
BARRY OR NOTTINGHAM SYSTEM	When this system is adopted the payment is in respect of all work performed in shifting the partings and the roads in the face, standing all props and flats set in the face, and gobbing and walling in gob all rubbish made in the face where there is room for it in the gob, at .	0	3	per ton
	When the total thickness of the seam, including the rashes underneath the seam, is below from 5 ft. to 4 ft. 10 in., the Barry System is considered to become impracticable, and the Still System will have to be adopted, but only when the change in thickness takes place over considerable areas.			

	Description of Work.	Rate. s. d.	
THICKNESS CLAUSE.	The minimum thickness of coal in the seam is to be regarded as 4 ft. 6 in. An extra payment of ½d. per ton for every inch below this thickness is payable.		
CLOD.	In Barry work, clod above coal, and rashes under coal, to be added together and paid for at 0·36d. per ton per inch after the first six inches, which are to be included in the cutting price of the coal. In Stall work, the rashes will be cut in the roads and paid for as bottom.		
	Note.—The first six inches of Top Clod on the road must be paid for as rippings; the remainder to be paid as arranged for in the Schedule.		
CLEANING COAL, ETC.	Cleaning the Coal and shifting and gobbing the stones in the coal up to three inches in thickness 1½d. per ton; when they exceed three inches in thickness, the excess thickness to be paid for on the clod scale.		
	Note.—The 1½d. will be payable under any circumstances.		
CUTTING BOTTOM IN BARRY FACES	When it becomes necessary to cut bottom through the Barry Faces by reason of the thinness of the section, such bottom will become payable per yard forward, at . . .	0 1½	per inch
DOUBLE SHIFT IN BARRY ROAD AND STALLS.	On night coal, when instructed by the Management to do so . . .	0 3	per ton
HEADINGS	Narrow, single turn	7 1	per yard
	Wide, through faces	4 11	,,
	Main Level Headings . . .	4 11	,,
	Double turns in Headings . . .	2 7·5	,,
	Treble shifts in Headings . . .	5 3	,,
	Barry or Nottingham Roads . .	1 9	,,
	Temporary Roads, unless exceeding 12 yards in length	Nil	
	Temporary Roads, exceeding 12 yards in length to be paid for from the turning	1 9	,,
	All Headings and Barry Roads to be 12 ft. wide.		
AIRWAY.	Airway	3 0	,,
	Walling sides of Headings, for each side	0 4	,,
	Note.—A deduction of one yard to be made for each cog.		
TIMBER.	Timber 9 ft.	2 4	per pair
	Timber 6½ ft.	1 9	,,
	Flats	1 6	,,
	Cogs	2 0	each
	Repairing Posts	0 6	,,
	Props out (unbroken)	0 3	,,

	Description of Work.	Rate. s. d.	
TIMBER—*Cont.*	Props out (broken)	0 1·5	each
UNLOADING.	Unloading and Walling Rubbish	0 6	per tram
	Filling Rubbish	0 6	,,
	Shifting Rubbish	0 6	,,
	Filling Water	0 6	per cask
WASTE.	When walled from bottom to top, keeping a clear space of from 3 to 4 ft. between coal and gob	0 9	per yard
	Turning Stall	6 0	
	Rib adjoining boundary barrier, or when instructed by the Management, but no Rib to be paid for when Heading price is paid on road	1 6	,,
	Ripping top or cutting bottom in headings, levels or Nottingham Road, 7 ft. wide, per inch per yard	0 2·5	
	Ripping top or cutting bottom in stalls not less than 5 ft. wide, per inch per yard	0 2·2	
	Note.—One flat to be paid for each side of a Barry Road, each shifting of face throughout, when necessary, otherwise two posts each side.		
	When special timbering becomes necessary in the face other than the ordinary flats and posts, such timbering work is to be paid for extra as per list, when set up, and lagged by specific direction of the Management.		
DAYWORK.	Daywork as per 9 ft. List. Customs and practices operating in 6 ft. and 9 ft. seams to apply to this seam.		

II

THE BOARD OF CONCILIATION AND ARBITRATION FOR THE BOOT AND SHOE TRADE OF NORTHAMPTON

STATEMENT FOR LASTING AND FINISHING THE BRITISH ARMY ANKLE BOOT agreed between the Northampton Boot Manufacturers' Association and the No. 1 Northampton Branch of the Boot Operatives' Union, December 2, 1916.

LASTING

	Per doz. prs.
Tacking-up backs, stiffeners properly prepared, one tack	2¼d.
Ditto, two tacks	2½d.
Rex pull-over, without toe-puff	3¼d.
Ditto, with toe-puff, operator to position puff	3¾d.
Jointing, after Rex, four places	3d.
Consol lasting, properly jointed, B.U. B-5	8¼d.
Ditto, Reg. No. 2	8¾d.
Rex pounding-up	3d.
Attaching through-middles, eight places	2¾d.

	Per doz. prs.
Cutting string and slipping off, hinge last	2d.
Ditto, block last	2½d.
Loose-nailing	3¼d.
Sole attaching, eight tacks	2¾d.
Ditto, with piece-sole	3¼d.
Stitching, Model M.	3½d.
Ditto, Rapid	5d.
Screwing all round, as per sealed pattern, New Rapid	3d.
Ditto, other	3¾d.
Levelling Machine, Hercules	1¾d.

All bench work according to shop arrangement.

Finishing

As to heels, when heel is attached—

	Per doz. prs.
Breasting and clearing, one operation (not less than 80 per cent must be cleared)	1¼d.
Breasting only	¾d.
Clearing only	1d.
Heel-trimming and randing	1¾d.
Ditto, not randed	1¼d.

Edge-trimming—

Starting from a minimum of 5¼d. per dozen pairs, there shall be an advance of one halfpenny per dozen pairs, with the exception of those houses already paying 7½d. per dozen pairs, and upwards.

Rough and fine heel-scouring	4d.
Seat-wheeling	1⅜d.
Padding, heels to be coloured	1⅜d.
Edge-setting, colour own work	7d.
Ditto, not coloured	6d.

All other operations to be left to present shop arrangements.

General Conditions

1. The Statement is for operatives 18 years of age and upwards.

2. It is decided that the Army Statement shall come into work December 11, and that Shop Statements for civilian work shall be fixed up in each factory to work along with the Army Statement, but as it is anticipated that all factories will not be ready for civilian Shop Statements by that date, workers are asked not to wait for same, as it is agreed that efforts shall be mutually made to fix up all Shop Statements for civilian trade by the end of the year. Any moneys earned above wages received on the basis of such Statement when fixed up, shall be paid from the full week commencing December 11. As, and when Statements are mutually agreed upon at the various factories, employees can commence working to same forthwith.

3. It is agreed that the Statements are to be worked to on the supplementary wage principle, viz. that all workers shall receive not less than their present wages for 52½ hours' work weekly, and all work done in excess of the agreed rates for wages received shall be paid for accordingly.

4. It is agreed that this is a weekly and not a daily Statement. Also, that a worker shall not be penalised for a break-down in machinery if he is kept in the factory.

5. That the War Bonus paid during this period is to be counted as an extra, and not as part of wages in calculating totals and earnings.

III

SOME TYPICAL PRICE LISTS

A. Cotton

The Oldham Spinners' List.
The Bolton Spinners' List.
The Blackburn List for Slubbing, Intermediate and Roving.
The Universal List for Flat Cards (Card-room Operatives).
The Universal List for Frames (Card-room Operatives).
The Uniform List for Weaving.
The Colne Coloured Goods List (Weavers).

B. Other Textiles

The Huddersfield Woollen Weavers' List.
The Leicester Hose List.
The Leicester Shirts, Pants, Dresses, Vests, and Trousers List.
The Leicester Trimmers' Price List.
The Nottingham Lace Trade Lists.
The Macclesfield Silk Trade List.
The Kidderminster Brussels Carpet List.
The Leicester Elastic Web List.
The Bradford and Halifax Slubbing Dyeing List.

C. Boots and Shoes

Northampton Statement for Lasting and Finishing the British Army Ankle Boot.
Kettering Men's M.S. Lasting Statement.
Leicester No. 3 (Women's) Statement for Closing.
Leicester No. 1 Piece-work Statement for Lasting Machines.
London Uniform Statement.
Northampton Clickers' Quantity Statement.
Manchester Hand-sewn Boot Trade Statement.
Amalgamated Union of Co-operative Employees' National Minimum Statement for Boot Repairers.

D. Clothing

London Time Log (Dress and Frock Coats).
Blackburn Machine Log.
Denton List of Prices for Fur and Wool Hats.

E. Printing

The London Scale of Prices for Compositors' Work (Book, Jobbing, Parliamentary, and News).
Typographical Association Linotype Machine Rules.
Typographical Association Monotype Keyboard Rules.
London Minimum List of Prices for Piece-work Case-making (Bookbinders).

F. Transport

Coal Trimming and Bunkering Rates (all districts. Transport Workers' Federation.)
London Timber Porters' List.
Bristol Grain-Porters' List.
London Stevedores' List (general cargoes).

G. Woodworking

Burton-on-Trent Coopers' List.
Liverpool Coopers' List.

H. Glass

Yorkshire Glass Bottle Makers' List.

I. Mining

Numerous Pit and Seams Lists from South Wales, Yorkshire, Derbyshire, etc.
Also Lists for Limestone Quarries, etc.

J. Iron and Steel

North of England Puddlers' List.
South Wales Tinplate Trade List.

K. Shipbuilding

Clyde Riveters' List.
Tyne and Wear Riveters' List.
Belfast Caulkers' List.
Hebburn (Messrs. Hawthorn, Leslie) Drillers' List.
North Shields (Edward Brothers) Hand Drillers' List.

L. Miscellaneous Metal Trades

South Staffordshire Wrought Nail Trade List.
South Staffordshire Nut and Bolt Trade List.
Chain-makers' Admiralty Chain List.
London Tin and Iron Ware, Baths, etc., List.

M. Brushmaking

London Brushmakers' List.

N. Building

Leicester Slaters' and Tilers' List.

Note.—A long list of piece-work statements and price lists in operation in 1910 is included in the Board of Trade Report on *Collective Agreements* published in that year (Cd. 5366).

APPENDIX G

THE GRADING OF LABOUR

We saw in the first chapter of this book that in certain cases an attempt is made to apply the principle of Labour "grading," *i.e.* to grade the various classes of workers in accordance with their varying degrees of skill. Such a system, we saw, prevails to a slight extent in certain branches of the furnishing trades. It has, however, been developed into a definite and comprehensive system, fully sanctioned by collective agreement, only in one case that has come to my notice. This case is that of the Birmingham brass trades; and it deserves separate exposition if only on account of the importance attached to it by some of those who have had experience of its working. I take the account of it *verbatim* from Mr. W. A. Dalley's *Life Story of W. J. Davis*, which is now out of print: [1]

"The workmen are graded into seven classes, these classes being denoted by different coloured adhesive stamps affixed to their membership cards, viz. yellow, green, brown, blue, grey, red, and mauve. The issue of these cards is in the hands of the Executive of the men's Society, and each card must be provided with suitable space for the workman's number at his works and in his Society, and also for his name and signature.

It has been suggested, and indeed it is ultimately hoped, that the issue of the grade cards will, in the near future, be made the joint duty of the Society and the manager of the Municipal Brass Trades School. This, if it can be brought about, will obviously be a most desirable thing, not only for the men but also for the trade. It would link up, as it were, the Technical School with the workshop. Surely a much needed reform not only in the brass trade but in many others.

Set out on following pages are the particulars of the seven grades or classes, together with the qualifications for each grade. It will be seen that the lowest grade (yellow) is for improvers of 21 years of age, and carries with it a minimum wage of 5½d. and a fraction per hour, or 25s. per week. The next grade (green) requires a three years' qualification, and the minimum for this is 6½d., less a fraction, per hour, or 27s. per week. So the men go on from grade to grade, until they reach the 'blue' grade with its 35s. per week, or the 'grey' grade, the minimum of which is 37s. per week. But this is not all, for provision is made for experts, and also for first-class experts. The former, known as the 'red' grade, includes dressers, art bronzers, chasers, patternmakers, burnishers, makers-up, and stampers, and to them is secured a minimum wage of 8⅝d. per hour, or 39s. per week. The latter grade (mauve), which by the way is confined to polishers, lays down a minimum of 41s. per week.

---

[1] *The Life Story of W. J. Davis, J.P.* (Birmingham Printers, Ltd., 1914. 3s. 6d.).

QUALIFICATIONS

A.—Yellow.

Improvers of 21 years of age.

Minimum wage, 5½d. and a fraction per hour, or per week 25s.

B.—Green Grade.

21 years of age. Three years' qualification in the trade.

Dressers who turn over plain work and are used to tapping and plate screwing and can file-over at the vice.

Polishers.—Those who have worked at their trade three years and who emery-bob, rough, or mop common work, and finish barrelled work.

Dippers.—Ordinary dippers and bronzers.

Burnishers who burnish tubes and common work at the lathe or vice.

Chasers and repairers who have had three years' continuous experience in the branch.

Semi-skilled makers-up who bend tubes by the block, file and tie on, and braze common and medium class work.

Stampers who run their own forces and stamp ordinary shallow work.

Minimum wage, 6⅛d. less a fraction per hour, or per week 27s. 6d.

C.—Brown Grade.

21 years of age, with four years' qualification in the trade.

Dressers who turn, screw inside and out, and file flat and true at the vice.

Polishers.—Those who have worked at their trade five years, and who either emery-bob, rough, or mop and finish any common work.

Dippers.—All-round dippers and bronzers.

Burnishers.—Advanced burnishers used to hook and straight burnishing on the vice and shell work on the lathe.

Chasers and repairers who chase and repair better-class work.

Makers-up who bend, file, fit, and solder better-class work.

Stampers who run their own forces and stamp deep shell work.

Minimum wage, 6⅞d. and a fraction per hour, or per week 31s.

D (1).—Blue Grade.

21 years of age, with six years' qualification in the trade.

Dressers who turn, screw inside and out, plug and seat, file flat and square at the vice, and finish their own work throughout.

Polishers.—Those who are experts in grades above, and do *all* (not any) of the above processes in common work ; those who do all the above processes in above grades, and emery-bob, and mop best work.

Dippers who qualify in the preceding grade, and also do art bronzing and colouring, or electro-plating, or have a knowledge of electro-plating and solutions.

Burnishers who are expert hook and straight burnishers at the vice, and satisfactorily burnish deep thin shell work at the lathe.

Chasers and repairers who properly chase and repair best work, and are experts at their trade.

Makers-up who have advanced knowledge and experience of all classes of the trade or branch in which they are employed.

Stampers who undertake all classes of deep or shallow work in all strengths of the metal used.

Minimum wage, 7¾d. and a fraction per hour, or per week 35s.

D (2).—Grey.

Polishers only. Those who rough or finish best work.

Minimum wage, 8¼d. less a fraction per hour, or per week 37s.

E (1).—*Red Grade.*

Dressers who have a complete expert knowledge and experience of all classes of lathe and vice work, or work to blue prints or drawings.

Art bronzers who have an expert knowledge of art bronzing or metal colouring, or electro depositing and solutions.

Chasers.

Patternmakers.

Burnishers who are experts in speed and quality in all classes of work.

Makers-up who make up best work throughout.

Stampers who are experts in all classes of work.

Minimum wage, 8⅝d. and a fraction per hour, or per week 39s.

E (2).—*Mauve.*

Polishers only.—First-class expert in all processes—in fact, a first-rate workman; or charge-hand, with duty of being responsible for all work, order, etc., in the shop.

Minimum wage, 9⅛d. less a fraction per hour, or per week 41s.

It has been seen in a previous chapter that the brass trades are most complex. Indeed, so complex that much difficulty was at first found in being able to enumerate the qualifications of every process or subdivision of the different branches of the industry. It is therefore to be understood that the qualifications set out above must, in some instances, serve only as a basis upon which the workman is graded. Provision in the scheme is therefore made for a workman's general usefulness as a member of the brass trade to receive consideration where and when such usefulness is served apart from his work as a specialist only.

The actual grading, as has already been pointed out, is done by the men's organisation. For this purpose a 'grading committee' of experts is annually appointed by the executive. Employers have the right to challenge the qualifications of the holder of any ticket, and require him to submit himself for examination by the managers of the Municipal Brass Trades School, in conjunction with a representative nominated by the Employers' Association, together with a representative nominated by the men's organisation. Should the decision be against the workman, it shall be at the discretion of the Society to put such workman down one grade; if, on the other hand, it be in favour of the workman, the employer shall pay a fee of 10s. to the Municipal Brass Trades School. In either event, however, the employer shall not be bound to reinstate the challenged workman.

The examination is conducted on practical lines, and includes the various processes in the workman's particular branch of the trade. The result of the challenge is, after the examination, endorsed on the workman's card, and, if three adverse decisions are endorsed, the workman automatically drops back one grade.

Any workman graded by the Society shall have the right to qualify for a higher grade, by submitting himself for examination by the before-mentioned authority, if required to do so by his employer. The same conditions prevail as in the case of an employer challenging the qualifications of a workman, and, should the decision be in favour of the workman, the 10s. fee is paid by the employer to the school. On the other hand, if the decision be adverse to the workman, the fee is paid by his Society, and the workman remains at least six months in the grade he was placed previous to the examination.

The grading committee has done its work well, and up to the present time employers have had to challenge the qualification of very few of their men. Truly an eloquent testimony to the care exercised in grading."

The question has often been raised whether it would be possible or desirable to extend this scheme to other trades. To Mr. W. J. Davis and his biographer, who was at one time Mr. Davis's Assistant Secretary in the National Society of Brassworkers, it stands for a new and important departure in methods of wage-payment. "If there is anything in industrial organisation," says Mr. Dalley, "more hated by Mr. Davis than the strike, it is probably what is known as the 'standard rate' without regard to individual merit and capacity. To him such a system stifles ambition and stultifies incentive—and, moreover, is bound, sooner or later, to have a disastrous effect on the trade itself, as well as a demoralising effect on the worker."

The "grading system," then, is put forward as an alternative to the standard rate, and as a means of supplying incentive. In this it closely resembles the various systems of payment by results, to which also it may be regarded as a possible alternative.

Such grading by means of collective bargaining is, as we saw, quite a different thing from individual grading of each worker by the employer, such as prevails in weakly organised trades. It is more like the very frequent practice of paying workers an advance on the standard rate for special work, *e.g.* in the tool-room. As long as inequality of remuneration persists at all within a trade, or as long as skilled and unskilled workers are paid at different rates, there would seem to be no objection in principle to further grading, provided that the number of grades remains small, and that the actual grading is carried out by the Unions themselves and fully safeguarded by collective bargaining. It is, however, doubtful whether the system is capable of ready adaptation over wide areas or to complicated trades or industries, though it is quite possible that it may spread in small trades and in individual establishments. It may even, in conjunction with other principles, form an element in the method of fixing and adjusting remuneration in the future even in so complicated an industry as engineering. It would indeed, even in that case, be largely a regularisation and extension of a method which already prevails widely in an unregulated form in the case of special classes of work.

SELECTED BOOK-LIST

A. General

COLE, G. D. H. *Workshop Organisation.*
SCHLOSS, D. F. *Methods of Industrial Remuneration.*
WEBB, S. AND B. *Industrial Democracy.*
WEBB, S. *The Works Manager To-day.*
ATKINSON, H. *A Rational Wages System.*
ATKINSON, H. *Co-operative Production.*
CADBURY, G. *Experiments in Industrial Organisation.*
ASHLEY, W. J. *The Adjustment of Wages.*
TAWNEY, R. H. *Minimum Rates in the Tailoring Industry.*
BRASSEY AND CHAPMAN. *Work and Wages.*
The Engineer. The Premium System of Paying Wages.
W. ROWAN THOMPSON. *The Rowan Premium Bonus System.*
J. E. PROSSER. *Piece-rate, Premium, and Bonus.*
F. W. LANCHESTER. *Industrial Engineering.*
Trades Union Congress. *The Premium Bonus System : Report of an Inquiry.*
Board of Trade. *Report on Standard Piece-Rates.* (Out of print.)
Board of Trade. *Report on Collective Agreements.* Cd. 5366. 1910.
Committee on Industry and Trade. *Report on Industrial Relations.* 1926.
United States Bureau of Labour Statistics. *Regulation and Restriction of Output.*
D. A. McCABE. *The Standard Rate in American Trade Unions.*
H. B. BUTLER. *Industrial Relations in the United States.* (Geneva, 1927.)
United States Government. *Report of the Commission on Industrial Relations.* 1915. (Final Report.)

B. Scientific Management and Industrial Psychology

R. F. HOXIE. *Scientific Management and Labour.*
F. W. TAYLOR. *The Principles of Scientific Management.*
F. B. COPLEY. *Frederick W. Taylor.*
C. B. THOMPSON. *Scientific Management.*
H. B. DRURY. *Scientific Management.*
HARRINGTON EMERSON. *Efficiency.*
F. B. GILBRETH. *Motion Study.*
F. B. GILBRETH. *Primer of Scientific Management.*
F. B. GILBRETH. *Applied Motion Study.*
H. L. GANTT. *Work, Wages and Profits.*
M. AND A. M'KILLOP. *Efficiency Methods.*
F. WATTS. *An Introduction to the Psychological Problems of Industry.*
C. S. MYERS. *Mind and Work.*
C. S. MYERS. *Industrial Psychology in Great Britain.*
B. MUSCIO. *Lectures in Industrial Psychology.*
P. S. FLORENCE. *Economics of Fatigue and Unrest.*
H. M. VERNON. *Industrial Fatigue and Efficiency.*
O. TEAD. *Instincts in Industry.*
R. B. WOLF. *Modern Industry and the Individual.*
S. A. LRWISOHN. *The New Leadership in Industry.*
Reports of the *Health of Munition Workers' Committee* and the *Industrial Fatigue Research Board.*

INDEX

THE END

Printed in Great Britain by R. & R. CLARK, LIMITED, *Edinburgh.*

For Product Safety Concerns and Information please contact our EU representative GPSR@taylorandfrancis.com Taylor & Francis Verlag GmbH, Kaufingerstraße 24, 80331 München, Germany